Business English
and Conversation
for the EFL-ESL Classroom

A combination textbook-workbook on Business English, Conversation and Correspondence for students of EFL (English as a Foreign Language) or ESL (English as a Second Language)

Armando Aceituno M.

Business English and Conversation for the EFL-ESL Classroom

Layout : Black Angel Enterprises

Editing and Proofreading: Servitec

1st published by
Universal Publishers/uPUBLISH.com
USA • 2000

ISBN: 1-58112-712-X

www.upublish.com/books/aceituno.htm

INTRODUCTION

Recent developments in technology, plus the world of globalization have caused our classrooms to change substantially. Nowadays, the teacher needs to understand a lot more about technology than he/she used to. It is not enough to be fluent in the English language to be able to teach it. If you do not possess the skills that this new world and new millenium require, you will be hopelessly left behind.

This Business English and Conversation book was created thinking about the specific needs of the ESL-EFL teachers and their students. It is meant to serve as a useful guide to aid in the development of the fluency needed in and out of the classroom.

Because of the grammar and correspondence requirements of our world, this modernized and up-to-date series offers these characteristics:

◈ General exercises which help the students develop all four basic skills:

✓ **Listening**   ✓ **Speaking**
✓ **Reading**   ✓ **Writing**

◈ Grammar practice and reviews
◈ A correspondence section with varied samples of the common business documents.
◈ Business, Internet, data processing and general vocabulary
◈ Optional conversation, writing and spelling exercises
◈ General reviews and recycling of all material.

As is the case with most other works of this nature, this book is as complete as humanly possible, but it can still use your helpful suggestions on how to make it better. Please send your comments or questions either to grandowner@yahoo.com or flacapuntas@hotmail.com.

Armando Aceituno M.

ABOUT THIS BOOK

Some reference works define Business English as the **correct and proper way** to use the language. But how can you use the language properly unless you know it well from its foundation?

Think of it this way:

> When you build a house, what do you build first? Do you install the roof before the foundation? Never. You lay the foundation first.

That's also the way to build correct habits on using the language, from its very own foundation.

This book does exactly that. It begins from the foundations of language: the **parts of speech.** It goes into each and every one of them in a brief yet comprehensive way, from the simple ones like **nouns** to the more complex ones like **auxiliary verbs.** Then it goes into using those parts of speech correctly in **sentences.**

Once you know how to use the parts of speech in **sentences**, we will go into some important items such as tag questions, conditions with if, capitalization, and punctuation marks. You will then be ready to start building **paragraphs** that make sense and accomplish their objective. Afterwards, you can go into making effective business **documents.**

Furthermore, as you progress by doing the required and optional exercises in the book, you will be putting your conversational skills to work.

The section on **correspondence** also begins from the simple **parts of the letter**, then goes into all the different **styles** and **types of letters.** Samples of each type of letter are included, as well as exercises to help you put your writing skills at work.

How can you best use the book to your advantage?

It depends on your own situation. Therefore, carefully analyze your needs before you begin, then adapt the book to suit those needs, not the other way around. **Business English and Conversation** has been developed based on past experiences with groups of all types and levels, but it is up to you to use it in the way that you best think fit.

What we did not include:

Pronunciation: The English language pronunciation cannot be written, unless we use the international symbols which have been designed and created specifically for that purpose. This is because English has more than 40 recognized sounds, many of which do not exist in other languages. Therefore, it is extremely difficult to write the pronunciation even of simple words like **CUT**. The sound of the letter **U** in **CUT** is pronounced in a way which cannot be accurately represented with the basic alphabet. In addition to this, it is a known fact that good pronunciation can best be learned by **listening** to the teacher and other speakers of the language.

About the author

Armando Aceituno M. has been teaching ESL and EFL for over twenty years.

A textbook author, teacher trainer, lecturer, novelist, poet, playwright and screenwright, he has published more than twenty five books for teachers and students of ESL and EFL. His textbooks have been used at hundreds of schools located in several areas of his native Latin America. He has also published poetry, short stories, and manuals on diverse computer programs.

His EFL-ESL works include:

- ❖ Bilingual Dictionary - English/Spanish
- ❖ Better English Today, *Books 1, 2 and 3*
- ❖ TOEFL Workshop - A Practical Approach
- ❖ Commercial English and Correspondence
- ❖ Freedom, *Books 1, 2 and 3*
- ❖ English Magic, *Books 1-6*
- ❖ English Power, *Books 1, 2 and 3*
- ❖ English Control, *Books 1, 2 and 3*
- ❖ English Literature for the EFL-ESL classroom
- ❖ EFL-ESL Teachers' Handbook, *under production*

Table of Contents

PART I – GRAMMAR

PART II – CORRESPONDENCE

PART I

Structure

and

Conversation

PARTS OF
SPEECH

English, like most structured languages, has a strong foundation: the parts of speech.

The main parts of speech are:

Nouns	**Pronouns**	**Adjectives**
Adverbs	**Prepositions**	**Conjunctions**
Interjections	**Verbs**	

Look at this example:

For Christmas, my sister gave me a computer and some very nice programs. Great!

The example above contains most of the main parts of speech:

NOUNS	: Christmas, sister, computer, programs
PRONOUN	: me
ADJECTIVES	: my, some, nice
CONJUNCTION	: and
ADVERB	: very
PREPOSITION	: for
VERB	: gave
INTERJECTION	: Great!

It also has an ARTICLE : "a"

Are parts of speech important? **They are essential!** Without them, we don't have a language and we can't communicate.

PREPOSITIONS

Nouns

Adjectives

Pronouns

Adverbs

Verbs

Conjunctions

We all need to know what the parts of speech are, but more important than that, we must know how to use them correctly.

This entire section of the book will teach you what each part of speech is and how to use it well. We'll begin by looking at nouns.

 READING AND CONVERSATION PRACTICE
Read, in pairs or individually, the following dialogue.

A: I think parts of speech are important.
B: Why?
A: Because most languages have them.
B: That doesn't prove anything.
A: Yes, it does.
B: What does it prove?
A: It proves their importance in everyday communication.

Now, complete the dialogue below with any appropriate words. Some spaces may have more than one possible answer. Share with your teacher or classmates when you are done.

A: Do you _____ parts of speech are _____?
B: Yes, I _____.
A: Why?
B: Because _____ languages have them.
A: What does that _____?
B: Their importance in everyday _____.

Chapter 1 — Nouns

Nouns are the most common words in the language, because they **identify everything** that surrounds us.

Nouns give name to people, things, places, animals, and ideas or concepts.

PEOPLE
Louise
uncle
sister
brother
nurse

THINGS
liquid
Internet
car
tower
monitor

PLACES
market
Mexico
office
world
bookstore

ANIMALS
eagle
frog
kangaroo
butterfly
tiger

CONCEPTS
peace
love
boredom
anxiety
happiness

Nouns have several characteristics.
Among others, they can sometimes be masculine, feminine, or neutral. They can also be singular, plural, proper, common, and can even specify number.

MASCULINE	FEMININE	NEUTRAL	NUMBER
man	girl	president	unicorn
lion	lioness	Internet	bicycle
prince	princess	doctor	triplets
bull	cow	secretary	quartet
steward	stewardess	program	pentathlon
actor	actress	computer	octopus

Business English and Conversation - Armando Aceituno M.

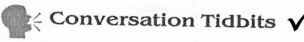

Conversation Tidbits ✓

A. Explain the following terms orally or in writing.

Internet _____

_____

boredom_____

_____

anxiety_____

_____

pentathlon_____

_____

concept _____

_____

B. With a partner or in groups, discuss the following terms. As an option, you might also want to use them in complete and correct sentences.

essential	importance	surround	lioness
triplets	unicorn	tower	steward

D. Optional Conversation Practice. With a partner or in groups, create and present a brief dialogue in which you use several feminine nouns.

C. Answer the following questions orally or in writing.

What is a noun?

_____

_____

Why are nouns important?

_____

_____

What characteristics do nouns have?

_____

_____

Do you think nouns have the same characteristics in all languages? Why?

_____

_____

What characteristics do nouns have in your native language?

_____

_____

Now, complete the paragraph below with any appropriate words. Some spaces may have more than one possible answer.

Nouns are _____ in every language. They _____ names to people, things, objects, and _____ . They serve to remind us what it is that we _____ facing, owning, obtaining, etc. And since nouns _____ the names of every thing that surrounds us, they do _____ in all the languages of the world. A world without nouns would not be a _____ at all.

Business English and Conversation - Armando Aceituno M.

Proper and Common Nouns

Proper nouns talk about a specific person, thing, animal or place. They should always begin with a capital letter.

Common nouns are not specific and are not capitalized unless they begin a sentence or phrase.

PROPER
NOUNS

Paula
Los Angeles
Wall Street
Channel 7
Belmont High School

COMMON
NOUNS

keyboard
glass
printer
telephone
mouse

Let's practice. If the noun is proper, write "P". If it is common, write "C".

1. _____Alice
2. _____mother
3. _____niece
4. _____Ronald
5. _____accountant
6. _____Guatemala
7. _____turkey
8. _____McDonald's
9. _____hippo
10. _____mouse

11. _____snow
12. _____Denver
13. _____box
14. _____book
15. _____Marie
16. _____Beverly
17. _____lion
18. _____hospital
19._____Regional Hospital
20. _____park

Optional Writing Practice: Write 5 common nouns and 5 proper nouns.

COMMON	PROPER
1. _____	1. _____
2. _____	2. _____
3. _____	3. _____
4. _____	4. _____
5. _____	5. _____

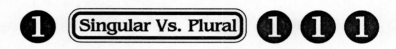

Singular Vs. Plural

Most nouns have a singular form and a plural form. There are some very strict rules that must be followed when we write the plural form. However, there are so many exceptions to some of these rules, that your best bet would be to use a good dictionary when you are not sure how a word is spelled.

In most cases, all you need to do is add an "S" to the singular form.

hat	**hats**	control	**controls**
race	**races**	eye	**eyes**
farm	**farms**	boy	**boys**

Some nouns that end in "o" add "es", while others add only "s".

hero	**heroes**	tomato	**tomatoes**
patio	**patios**	shampoo	**shampoos**

When a noun ends in "y" preceded by a consonant, the "y" is changed into "i" then "es" is added.

diary   diaries   story   stories

But, if the noun ends in "y" after a vowel, then we just add "s".

play   plays   toy   toys

When the noun ends in X, Z, SH, CH, or S, you need to add "ES" to form the plural.

| ash | ashes | box | boxes |
| watch | watches | class | classes |

If the noun ends in "f" or "fe", we usually change the ending to "ves".

| wife | wives | life | lives |
| loaf | loaves | knife | knives |

However, there are many exceptions to this rule:

| safe | safes | cuff | cuffs |
| chief | chiefs | roof | roofs |

We also find some nouns which have irregular plural forms.

child	children	ox	oxen
man	men	woman	women
mouse	mice	louse	lice
tooth	teeth	foot	feet
die	dice	fungus	fungi
goose	geese	pensum	pensa

Last but not least, there are nouns which use the same form in singular or plural:

sheep   deer   moose   buffalo   fish

"Fish" uses the same form when it
refers to fish of the same species.
When we talk about different species,
then we use the form "fishes."

Practice A.   Write the plural form of each noun.

1. play_____   11. toy _____

2. woman_____   12. sinner_____

3. cliff_____   13. church_____

4. class_____   14. secretary_____

5. match_____   15. box _____

6. symbol_____   16. wife_____

7. louse_____   17. ledger_____

8. sentence_____   18. mouse_____

9. grape_____   19. dish_____

10. boot_____   20. foot_____

Optional Pronunciation Practice – Read aloud all the words
from Practice A.

**Optional Conversation Practice - Select
five words from Practice A and use them
in sentences or in a short dialogue with a
partner.**

Business English and Conversation - Armando Aceituno M.

Conversation Tidbits ✓

Practice A. How many different nouns can you spot in each picture?

Practice B. Write any plural nouns you see here.

Practice C. Write all the common nouns you find.

Optional. Discuss the photographs. In which continent do you think each place is located? Any idea as to the specific countries?

Practice B: If the noun is proper, write "P". If it is common, write "C".

1. _____ Lake Elsinore   6. _____ Nail Corporation

2. _____ street   7._____ U.S. Government

3. _____ church   8. _____ noun

4. _____ First National Bank   9. _____ directory

5. _____ nail   10. _____ Jennifer

Optional Conversation Practice – Explain to your classmates what the following terms mean: sinner, church, symbol, louse, ledger.

Optional Spelling Practice – Spell aloud the plural form of the following nouns: child, ox, man, woman, mouse, louse, tooth, die, fungus, goose.

Optional Reading and Writing Practice – Look up the meanings of the following words: ledger, symbol, cliff, die (*noun*), fungus, pensive, update, mainframe. Write the meanings in the space provided. Afterwards, discuss them with a partner or in groups.

ledger

_____

_____

symbol

_____

_____

die

_____

_____

fungus

_____

_____

pensive_____

_____

update_____

_____

mainframe_____

_____

Indefinite Article "A"

As you probably remember, we use "an" before vowels, silent "h" or short "u."

an asterisk	an orange
an upgrade	an honest man
an ugly man	an apple

"A" is used before a consonant or the long "u" sound:

a diskette	a tape	a directory
a horse	a united family	a symbol
a union	a university	a keyboard

21

Practice A - Write "a" or "an" before each noun.

1. _____ outstanding boy
2. _____ account
3. _____ evening
4. _____ chat club
5. _____ night

6. _____ index
7. _____ e-mail
8. _____ assistant
9. _____ university
10. _____ box

 Conversation Tidbit

Explain to your classmates what the following terms mean:
united, outstanding, chat club, e-mail, symbol.

Optional Spelling Practice – Your teacher will select several words from the previous pages for you to spell aloud..

How many more nouns can you connect?

			a					
			s					
			s					
			i	n	d	e	x	
			s					
			t					
			a					
			n					
			t					

Mass Nouns - Count Nouns

1. Mass nouns are those that can't be counted. With Mass Nouns we use **Much.**

MASS = She has more cake than I.   (A larger portion)
COUNT = She has more cakes than I. (More whole cakes)

Some mass nouns:

water	rice	coffee	homework
sugar	love	beef	gasoline
work	peace	trust	confidence

2. Count nouns can be counted. With these, we use **Many.**
Some count nouns:

cups	glasses	pieces	teaspoons
plates	meals	doors	marbles
hands	boxes	wishes	thoughts

Some nouns can be used in either way depending on the sentence. Sometimes we can use **HOW MANY** with count nouns if we add a unit of measure.

HOW MANY   glasses of water..   teaspoons of sugar...
          ounces of oil...   cups of coffee...

Practice A. Underline the mass nouns in the following sentences.

    1. How much oil do you need?
    2. Do you have some sugar left?
    3. Would you like some hot pepper sauce?
    4. Please bring me some ketchup.
    5. We don't have any salt.
    6. Did you buy the vinegar?
    7. Don't forget the pepper.
    8. Let's buy some milk.
    9. Bring me some juice, please.
    10. Would you like some beef?

Practice B. With the help of your teacher, match the mass nouns with an appropriate unit of measure. Some mass nouns may use the same unit or use more than one.

(___) milk   a. bag

(___) water   b. sack

(___) salt   c. cup

(___) beans   d. litter

(___) rice   e. gallon

(___) ketchup   f. package

(___) tea   g. ounce

(___) wine   h. glass

                        i. bottle

Notice the use of FEWER, LESS, and AS... AS:

I have fewer marbles than you.
You have fewer socks than I.   **COUNT NOUNS**
She has fewer friends than we.

I have less coffee than you.
You have less chicken than I.   **MASS NOUNS**
She has less salt than we.

I have as many marbles as you.
You have as many shoes as I.   **COUNT NOUNS**
She has as many friends as we.

I have as much coffee as you.
You have as much chicken as I.   **MASS NOUNS**
She has as much salt as we.

FEWER should be used with **count** nouns.
LESS should be used with **mass** nouns.
AS... AS can be used with both types of nouns.

Practice C. Complete each blank with FEWER or LESS as appropriate. Some sentences may have more than one possible answer.

1. She has _____ cassettes than I.

2. She has _____ romantic music than you.

3. You own _____ records than he.

4. He possesses _____ CD's than we.

5. We buy _____ classical music than they.

6. They purchase _____ radios than I.

7. I listen to _____ comedy on the radio.

8. We watch _____ comedy shows on TV.

9. I like _____ violence on TV.

10. He prefers _____ villains in the movies.

Practice D. Complete each blank with MANY or MUCH as appropriate.

1. Debbie has as _____ cassettes as I do.

2. He enjoys as _____ shows as you.

3. She has as _____ romantic music as I.

4. He knows as _____ chess as you.

5. He possesses as _____ chess boards as we.

6. They listen to as _____ trash on the radio as we do.

7. I listen to as _____ news reports as I can.

8. We watch as _____ comedy shows as possible.

9. He prefers as _____ loving couples as possible.

10. He has seen as _____ love displayed as I.

Optional Practice: Read aloud the completed sentences from both exercises on this page. Discuss them with a partner or in groups.

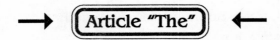

Article "The"

The article "THE" is not needed when we talk about some things in general.

People are strange.
Children like to play.
Trust is very important.

Love is wonderful.
Boredom is dangerous.
Computers are useful.

But most of the time we do need to use THE:

The boy likes to play.
The bus left already.
The people of Panama are nice.

The car won't start.
The computer is here.
The food is ready.

OTHER EXAMPLES:

With THE

The town

The computer

The file

The business (*a company or field of work*)

the message

the truth

the screen

Without THE

patience

freedom

justice

business (*in general*)

happiness

fun

liberty

If you are not a native speaker of the English language, it may be sometimes difficult to get used to when THE is needed. If you have doubts about the usage of this article, consult your teacher.

Business English and Conversation - Armando Aceituno M.

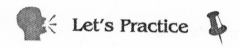

Let's Practice

Practice A - With the help of your teacher, write THE before each noun IF it is necessary.

1. _____ patience
2. _____ computer
3. _____ freedom
4. _____ children
5. _____ trust

6. _____ message
7. _____ town
8. _____ happiness
9. _____ people
10. _____ boredom

Optional Pronunciation Practice – Read all the words aloud.

Optional Conversation Practice – Explain to your class-mates what the following terms mean: patience, happiness, boredom, chat club, freedom, trust.

Optional Writing Exercise: Write in your notebook other nouns that DO NOT use the article THE.

Practice B. Use the following nouns in short sentences.

wife _____

ox _____

fungus_____

dice _____

sinner _____

Answer the following questions orally or in writing.

What is a proper noun?

_____

_____

What is a common noun?

_____

_____

Are proper nouns capitalized in your native language?

_____

Do nouns follow other rules in your native language?

_____

Explain:

_____

_____

There are many nouns in this picture. How many can you find?

Business English and Conversation - Armando Aceituno M.

Chapter 2 || Pronouns & Adjectives

Pronouns are words that replace one or more nouns.

Examples:

1. Becky knows that **she** is good looking.
2. Walter took his book home and left **it** there.

In Example 1, SHE is talking about Becky.
In Example 2, IT is talking about Walter's book.

In the following examples, what are the underlined pronouns referring to?

A. Michelle has stolen my heart and <u>**she**</u> likes that idea.
B. Why did you bring the car? **It** is not ready to be driven.

In Example A, SHE is talking about Michelle.
In Example B, IT is talking about the car.

The following sentences contain pronouns too. Can you find all of them? Circle the ones you find.

1. Give her the black purse.
2. She's looking at herself in the mirror.
3. It's a shame. He lost all his money last week.
4. Why did you bring him to the party?
5. Who do they think we are?
6. Whose books are those on the desk?
7. The man that I saw last night was your neighbor.
8. We'll buy the sweaters ourselves.

There are several kinds of pronouns:

SUBJECT PRONOUNS	OBJECT PRONOUNS	REFLEXIVE/ EMPHATIC PRONOUNS
I	me	myself
you (*singular*)	you	yourself
he	him	himself
she	her	herself
it	it	itself
we	us	ourselves
you (*plural*)	you	yourselves
they	them	themselves

INTERROGATIVE PRONOUNS	RELATIVE PRONOUNS
who	that
which	who
whom	which
what	whom
whose	whose

Subject Pronouns

These normally execute the action or perform the most important task in the sentence.

Examples:
1. **I** saved all my files on the diskette.
2. **They** faxed many documents
3. Does **he** have a new computer?
4. **She** goes home late after work.
5. **We** didn't take the typewriter.
6. When **you** arrived, **we** had already left.
7. **It** is important to save all your files.
8. Did **she** send the e-mail?

Object Pronouns

These receive the action.

Examples:

1. Brenda gives **me** a headache sometimes.
2. Peter sees **her** every week.
3. Alice told **us** about her behavior.
4. She said, "Take your money and put **it** away."
5. The diskettes are missing; Brian lost **them**.

Practice A. Underline <u>all</u> the pronouns used in the following sentences.

1. He saw the movie with her yesterday.
2. Why does Cindy hate him so much?
3. Where did she put it yesterday?
4. Did he center the pages?
5. David never completed the book, did he?.

Practice B. Circle only the <u>object</u> pronouns.

1. We saw him at the theater.
2. She told us to meet her later.
3. Where can I see you tomorrow?
4. He surprised them with that trick.
5. Think of me.

Optional Pronunciation Practice – Read aloud all sentences from Practice A.

Optional Reading and Writing Practice – Read sentences from Practice B in silence, then paraphrase them * orally or in your notebook.

* TO PARAPHRASE: To say the same thing but using different words.

31

Reflexive Pronouns

We use these to <u>reflect</u> the action back to the subject.

Nancy and Daniel saw **themselves** on TV.
Melissa cut **herself** with those scissors.
The radio can't turn **itself** on.
Eddie hurt **himself** last Saturday.
We are only lying to **ourselves.**

Practice C. Complete the following sentences with an appropriate reflexive pronoun, according to the subject of the sentence.

0. Michelle and I are angry with _____ .
0. Michelle and I are angry with ___OURSELVES___ .

1. Pablo saw _____ in the mirror.
2. Silvia and I saw _____ on the news.
3. Daniel and Karla hurt _____ .
4. We will laugh at _____ .
5. When did Frank cut _____ .
6. Why does Lizzy talk to _____ ?
7. Gladys always talks about _____ .
8. The teachers discussed it among _____ .
9. They really hate _____ now.
10. We should enjoy _____ at the party.

Optional Practice. How many sentences with pronouns can you write based on this picture?

<u>Example</u>:
They played their trumpets for us.

Business English and Conversation - Armando Aceituno M.

Emphatic Pronouns

Although these look like reflexive pronouns, they are used in a very different way.

1. Victor wrote this book without help. He wrote it **himself**.
2. My car broke down, but I repaired it **myself**.
3. Ericka planted the flowers **herself**, didn't she?
4. She wants me to explain the problem, but I don't understand it **myself**.

When we use emphatic pronouns, we <u>emphasize</u> the action that the subject is performing.

In Example 1 above, the pronoun means that Victor wrote the book without help from anyone. In Examples 2 and 3, the idea is also that no one helped the subject to perform the actions of repairing the car or planting the flowers. In Example 4, the pronoun means that the speaker does not understand the problem either.

Practice D. Circle only the <u>emphatic</u> pronouns in the following sentences.

1. Karen always looks at herself in the mirror.
2. Pietro himself washed the car.
3. Emily baked the cake by herself.
4. Johanna hates herself, doesn't she?
5. Stanley is hurting himself.
6. Why doesn't Walter wash the car himself?
7. Bill and Hector almost electrocuted themselves.
8. Mary and you destroyed the evidence yourselves.
9. Claudia herself washed the clothes.
10. They are listening to themselves.

Optional Practice – Paraphrase all sentences from Practice D.

33

Interrogative Pronouns

These are used to ask questions. They are:

who   which   whom   what   whose

Examples:
Which is your car?
Whom did you see last week?
What is the purpose for this meeting?
Who is that man?
Whose is this card?

Practice E. Complete the following sentences with any appropriate Interrogative Pronoun. Some sentences may have more than one possible answer.

1. _____ is the matter with you?
2. _____ is the creator of this project?
3. _____ is that folder on the desk?
4. _____ is the last one?
5. _____ do you like?

Relative Pronouns

These refer back to the subject or to another noun.

He has a car **that** I like. *(that refers to the car)*

The boy **whom** you met is a liar. *(whom refers to the boy)*

The girl **whose** book I have didn't come today. *(whose = the girl)*

William, **who** is inside, is my brother. *(who refers to William)*

The hat **which** I bought yesterday is torn. *(which refers to the hat)*

Business English and Conversation - Armando Aceituno M.

Reciprocal Pronouns

RECIPROCAL PRONOUNS are: <u>each other</u> and <u>one another</u>. Notice their use:

Paul and John are mad at each other.
They gave each other a present.
We forgave each other.
They seem to be in love with each other, don't they?
People should love one another.
The students wished good luck to one another.

<u>EACH OTHER</u> is normally used when we are talking only about two people.
<u>ONE ANOTHER</u> is used when we are talking about more than two people.

Practice F. Circle <u>all</u> the relative and interrogative pronouns.

1. Who are those people?
2. Which is your desk?
3. Whom did she select?
4. Whose are these folders?
5. What is the main reason?
6. Who is the lady in blue?
7. Which jacket did you bring?
8. What is the idea behind this?
9. The girl who called a few minutes ago is here.
10. The woman whose picture you took is angry.
11. The snake which I caught is poisonous.
12. Some people who complained were wrong.
13. The boy whom you like has a girlfriend.
14. The desk which you took wasn't mine.
15. The man whom I met scared me.

Optional Pronunciation or Conversation Practice — Read aloud the first ten sentences from Practice F or paraphrase them.

✎🗣≺Conversation Tidbits ✓

❶

Practice A. Write any common nouns you find in these illustrations.

Practice B. Discuss photograph 1. Where are these people? What are they doing? What do their facial expressions show? What might be the possible relationship between them? Would their social behavior be acceptable in your society? Why? Why not?

❷　　　　　　**❸**

Business English and Conversation - Armando Aceituno M.

Adjectives

Adjectives are words that can tell us many things about the noun. In other words, they modify the noun.

They can tell us <u>WHICH ONE, WHAT KIND, HOW MANY,</u> and most of the time must be placed before the noun.

<u>WHICH ONE?</u>	<u>WHAT KIND?</u>	<u>HOW MANY?</u>
That truck	**ripe** orange	**one** girl
those cars	**young** lady	**some** animals
this ocean	**honest** man	**several** guys
those faxes	**new** car	**thirteen** flags
this letter	**cute** baby	**many** numbers

This is why we say that adjectives can be descriptive, limiting, demonstrative, proper, or possessive.

Descriptive adjectives can tell us different things about a noun, such as consistency, temperature, speed, color, size, and appearance.

<u>CONSISTENCY</u>	<u>TEMPERATURE</u>	<u>SPEED</u>
thick mixture	**hot** milk	**fast** bike
soft paper	**warm** water	**slow** car
solid reason	**cold** ice	**quick** decision
hard head	**cool** person	**hasty** exit

<u>COLOR</u>	<u>SIZE</u>	<u>APPEARANCE</u>
yellow flower	**large** hand	**ugly** dog
pink lips	**short** boy	**handsome** man
gray shirt	**tiny** spot	**gorgeous** girl
blue pants	**tall** woman	**pretty** doll

Practice A. Write <u>any</u> appropriate adjective before each noun.

1. _____ desk
2. _____ e-mail
3. _____ program
4. _____ book
5. _____ dictionary
6. _____ mirror
7. _____ stapler
8. _____ paperclip
9. _____ show
10. _____ fingerprint

Optional Spelling Practice – Spell aloud the **nouns** from Practice A.

Optional Conversation Practice: Explain to your partner or classmates what the following phrases mean: hasty decision, gorgeous girl, solid reason, thick mixture, hard head

Limiting adjectives tell us quantity or order.

many items	**first** time	**second** call
some classes	**last** night	**twenty** laps
several seats	**fifteen** cakes	**fourth** corner

Practice B. Write any appropriate limiting adjective in the space provided.

1. __**several**__ people
2. _____ teams
3. _____ players
4. _____ gentleman
5. _____ soldiers

6. _____ fingers
7. _____ teeth
8. _____ tooth
9. _____ place
10. _____ medals

Business English and Conversation - Armando Aceituno M.

"To demonstrate" means "to show."
The **demonstrative adjectives** are:

SINGULAR	PLURAL
this	these
that	those

Their usage needs no further explanation, since they are such common words. However, it would be well to remember the following guidelines:

THIS and **THESE** are used when the object(s), person(s) or animal(s) we are talking about are close to the speaker.

THAT and **THOSE** are used when the object(s), person(s) or animal(s) we are talking about are far from the speaker.

Proper adjectives are specific and <u>always</u> CAPITALIZED.

German tourists   **Spanish** people
American ambassador   **New York** subway

Possessive adjectives are used to show <u>possession</u>. They are:

her happiness

my   its
your   our
his   their
her

Examples:

my friend   **our** people   **your** mother-in-law
his hand   **their** kids   **her** happiness
                   its case

39

Practice C. Write any appropriate adjective before each noun.

1. _____ cows
2. _____ women
3. _____ food
4. _____ socks
5. _____ toys

6. _____ wall
7. _____ hospital
8. _____ eyes
9. _____ light
10. _____ mom

Optional Conversation Practice. Use at least three of the nouns from Practice C in a short dialogue with a partner or in groups.

Comparison using Adjectives

We can use adjectives to make comparisons:

> Nancy is **tall**.
> Karla is **taller than** Nancy. She is the **taller** of the two.
> Evelyn is **taller than** Nancy and Karla.
> She is the **tallest** of the three.

The three forms of an adjective are the following:

POSITIVE	COMPARATIVE	SUPERLATIVE
fat	fatter (than)	the fattest
few	fewer (than)	the fewest
beautiful	more beautiful (than)	the most beautiful
old	older (than)	the oldest
honest	more honest (than)	the most honest
ugly	uglier (than)	the ugliest

To form the comparative and superlative forms of adjectives, we must follow certain rules. These rules are outlined in the following pages.

We add "er" to the adjective in its positive form and that changes it into its comparative form.

POSITIVE	COMPARATIVE	SUPERLATIVE
thick	thicker	thickest
dumb	dumber	dumbest

If the adjective ends in a consonant (except X, Z or W) preceded by one vowel, then we must double the last consonant before adding "er".

POSITIVE	COMPARATIVE	SUPERLATIVE
hot	hotter	hottest
fat	fatter	fatter

When the adjective ends in "e", we add only "r".

POSITIVE	COMPARATIVE	SUPERLATIVE
wise	wiser	wisest
large	larger	largest

If there is a final "y" preceded by a consonant, we change it into "i", then add "er".

POSITIVE	COMPARATIVE	SUPERLATIVE
pretty	prettier	prettiest
dirty	dirtier	dirtiest

Some adjectives have irregular forms.

POSITIVE	COMPARATIVE	SUPERLATIVE
good	better	the best
bad	worse	the worst
much	more/less	the most
many	more/less	the most/least
little (*mass nouns only*)	less/more	the least

41

When the adjective has more than one syllable, we normally use "more" to form the comparative and superlative forms.

POSITIVE	COMPARATIVE	SUPERLATIVE
beautiful	more beautiful	the most beautiful
honest	more honest	the most honest
intelligent	more intelligent	the most intelligent

Comparisons in Sentences

Look at the way we build sentences when we compare only two things. The comparative form of the adjective is used and, if needed, the conjunction "THAN".

Joseph is **younger than** Betty.
Karin looks **prettier than** Hellen.
Carlos is old, but Ronald looks **older**.

Practice D. Complete the following sentences using the comparative form of the adjective in parenthesis.

1. This program seems _____ . (complicated)

2. Your dog is _____ than mine. (smart)

3. That display is _____ . (expensive)

4. It sounds _____ . (loud)

5. My job is _____ than hers. (easy)

6. That file is _____ now. (messy)

7. Those names seem _____ . (long)

8. My car is _____ than yours . (sophisticated)

9. Dony seems _____ than Liz. (good)

10. A shark is _____ than a whale. (dangerous)

A. Underline the pronouns in the following sentences.

1. My brother gave me a nice surprise.
2. He brought a puppy with him.
3. It was a very cute dog. I liked it very much.
4. My mother, who doesn't like dogs, said she was scared.
5. We told her not to worry about the animal.

Optional Pronunciation Exercise. Read aloud the sentences from Practice A.

B. Complete the following sentences with the appropriate reflexive or emphatic pronoun.

1. Stephen_____ built that house.
2. I hit _____ with the hammer.
3. Carol and George moved the rock _____ .
4. Carmen is talking to _____ .
5. You and I will paint the wall _____ .

C. Circle or underline the <u>nouns</u> in the following list of words.

table	dinner	file	she
machine	listen	they	again
never	eye	luck	glass
eat	food	drinking	drunk
nose	small	we	chicken

Optional Spelling Exercise – Spell aloud the words from Practice C.

D. Write the appropriate reflexive pronoun for each subject.

SUBJECT	REFLEXIVE PRONOUN	SUBJECT	REFLEXIVE PRONOUN
1. my sister	_Herself_	9. a waiter	_____
2. your brother	_____	10. the restaurant	_____
3. my cats	_____	11. a nurse	_____
4. the boys	_____	12. the lion	_____
5. Yessie and I	_____	13. Dony and I	_____
6. the TV	_____	14. Walter	_____
7. You and I	_____	15. my father	_____
8. the reporters	_____	16. your children	_____

E. Write a synonym for each adjective. If your teacher allows it, you may use a dictionary.

1. thorough_____
2. lengthy_____
3. petite _____
4. puny _____
5. huge_____
6. somber_____
7. pale _____
8. cute _____
9. boyish_____
10. dense_____

11. moist_____
12. arid_____
13. ample_____
14. vital_____
15. upright_____
16. scrawny_____
17. unfair_____
18. musty_____
19. vast_____
20. nearby_____

F. Complete the following sentences with the comparative form of the adjective in parenthesis.

1. Is my car _____ than yours? (fast)
2. Your files are _____ than John's. (messy)
3. He is _____ now. (honest)
4. I think her office is _____ . (big)
5. Which is _____, Florida or Egypt? (hot)

Business English and Conversation - Armando Aceituno M.

G. Write the comparative form of each adjective.

COMPARATIVE

1. early_____
2. low_____
3. hard_____
4. wet_____
5. few_____
6. long_____
7. old _____
8. dirty_____

COMPARATIVE

9. dark _____
10. thin_____
11. hungry_____
12. big_____
13. short_____
14. smart_____
15. happy_____

H. Write the superlative form of each adjective.

SUPERLATIVE

1. thin _____
2. wide_____
3. few_____
4. good_____
5. confident_____

SUPERLATIVE

6. modest_____
7. white_____
8. many_____
9. warm_____
10. cool_____

I. Complete the following sentences with the superlative form of the adjective in parenthesis.

1. This is the _____ book here. (expensive)
2. I have the _____ house in Oregon. (large)
3. She is the _____ girl in town. (pretty)
4. We found the _____ rocks! (big)
5. Frank is the _____ human alive. (fast)

Optional Reading and Writing Practice – Read the completed sentences from Practice I in silence, then paraphrase them orally or in writing.

Conversation Tidbits ✓

Practice A. How many adjectives can you find in these photos? Write them all down.

Practice B. Discuss these photographs.
1. Are all these modes of public transportation?
2. Which ones are available in your country?
3. Which ones have you used?
4. Which ones would you rather not use? Why?

Business English and Conversation - Armando Aceituno M.

Chapter 3

A Few Not-so-Little Things

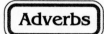 **Adverbs** These are words that modify verbs, adjectives or other adverbs

Adverbs that modify verbs:

He **seldom** comes home.   He left **early**.
She will learn **gradually**.   We found it **here**.

These adverbs can show manner, time, frequency or place where the action is done.

Some adverbs which can modify verbs:

Manner	Time	Frequency	Place
gradually	early	seldom	here
slowly	today	twice	there
easily	later	always	nowhere
quickly	soon	never	somewhere
carefully	yesterday	once	everywhere

Other Adverbs and Expressions of Frequency:

daily	often	frequently	weekly
monthly	rarely	thrice	usually
annually	ever	sometimes	seldom
most of the time			

Adverbs that modify adjectives tell us intensity or degree:

They are **really** mad.   She seems **rather** short.
He looks **very** angry.   The look **quite** ready to go.

Some adverbs which can modify adjectives:

extremely	incredibly	really	unbelievably
too	rather	very	quite

Adverbs that modify other adverbs can also tell us intensity or degree:

He ate **too** fast.   They sing **very** well.

Practice A. With the help of your teacher, write any appropriate adverb next to each verb, adjective, or adverb in the space provided.

1. _____ fast   6. _____ big

2. _____ fat   7. destroys _____

3. _____ thin   8. _____ bright

4. works _____   9. _____ intelligent

5. _____ easily   10. types _____

Adverbs can also be used in comparisons:

◆ A helicopter flies <u>fast</u>.
A plane flies <u>faster</u> than a helicopter.
The space shuttle flies the <u>fastest</u> of all.

Practice B. Write any appropriate adverb(s) in the space provided. Some spaces may have more than one correct answer.

1. Evelyn is a _____ beautiful woman.

2. She also works _____ well.

3. She likes to dress in _____ elegant clothes.

4. The first time I saw her, I liked her _____ much.

5. I love her _____.

Business English and Conversation - Armando Aceituno M.

Optional Reading and Writing Practice — Read the completed sentences from Practice B in silence, then paraphrase them in your notebook.

Optional Conversation Practice — Explain to your classmates what the following terms mean: carefully, later, expensive, unexpectedly, usually, organized, seldom.

Other adverbs and expressions of time are:

> already   still   yet   anymore   ago

ALREADY expresses an action that has been completed.

> Has he already arrived?   **Is he finished already?**
> I already ate my lunch.   **She already left.**

STILL expresses an on-going or continuous action.

> Do you still have my book?   **Yes, I still have it.**
> They are still working on that project. **He still loves her.**

YET expresses an action that has not been done or completed, but that is expected to be done or completed soon.

> Has she arrived yet?   **Have you finished it yet?**
> She hasn't arrived yet.   **I haven't finished it yet.**
> I have yet to see any results. **He has yet to tell me what to do.**

ANYMORE expresses actions which are no longer performed.

> I don't love her anymore.   **He doesn't work anymore.**

AGO expresses actions done in the past.

> How long ago did you see him?   **She left five years ago.**

Practice C. Complete the following sentences with the correct word from the parenthesis.

1. She left three days _____ . (yet, ago)
2. Have they brought the plans _____ ? (yet, ago)
3. They have _____ to tell us anything. (already, yet)
4. I don't smoke _____ . (still, anymore)
5. Are they _____ at school? (still, anymore)
6. Her eyes are _____ swollen. (still, anymore)
7. He doesn't like fish _____ . (still, anymore)
8. I have _____ seen them. (already, yet)
9. They haven't bought it _____ . (already, yet)
10. I saw her a few days _____ . (still, ago)

Practice D. Orally or in writing, make complete sentences with the adverb in parenthesis.

1. _____ (always)
2. _____ (frequently)
3. _____ (usually)
4. _____ (often)
5. _____ (sometimes)
6. _____ (seldom)
7. _____ (never)
8. _____ (daily)
9. _____ (weekly)
10 _____ . (monthly)

 Optional Spelling and Pronunciation Practice. Read aloud the adverbs which appear on this and previous pages. Spell them aloud as well.

Practice E. Answer the following questions:

1. What is the difference between ALREADY and YET?

_____

_____

_____

2. What's the proper use of AGO?

_____

_____

_____

3. What does STILL express?

_____

_____

Practice F. Complete each sentence with the appropriate word from the parenthesis.

1. _____ he still sleeping? (Is, It's)
2. I can't see him _____ . (still, yet)
3. It was six weeks _____ that she called. (ago, already)
4. They are _____ thinking about it. (yet, still)
5. They have _____ to reach a decision. (yet, already)
6. Has anybody been here _____ ? (yet, already)
7. Everybody has _____ gone home. (yet, already)
8. We don't go out _____ . (still, anymore)
9. She is _____ looking at herself. (still, anymore)
10. _____ easy to remember your face. (It's, Is)

Practice G. Complete each sentence with the appropriate adverb from the parenthesis.

1. He performed _____ well. (very, tomorrow)
2. She looks _____ short! (carefully, so)
3. They are _____ interested. (later, really)
4. We _____ found it. (never, very)
5. That computer is _____ expensive. (very, here)
6. My files are _____ organized. (well, today)
7. Ben _____ comes home at night. (here, usually)
8. He is _____ late. (today, seldom)
9. I'll show you the program _____ . (now, very)
10. The auditor showed up _____ . (so, unexpectedly)

Optional Conversation Practice. Paraphrase the completed sentences from Practice G, orally or in writing.

Practice H. Write any appropriate adverb. Some spaces may have more than one correct answer.

1. We have three _____ efficient secretaries.
2. Mary, the youngest, types _____ fast.
3. Evelyn, Mary's sister, types _____ than Mary.
4. But Dony types the _____ of all.
They don't like to work overtime.
5. Dony _____ stays after 6:00 pm.
6. Mary stays _____ than Dony.
7. Evelyn stays _____ of all.
8. We are _____ satisfied with them.
9. They do a _____ good job.

Prepositions

Prepositions are tricky words that show relationships between other words or the position of objects, people or animals. A lot of practice is needed in order to learn to use prepositions correctly in English.

With prepositions, we form the Prepositional Phrases. These are phrases that begin with a preposition and end with a noun or pronoun.

Examples:
He gave the food **to her.**   We bought it **for them.**
She ate it **in her office.**   He has the PC **in the room.**

Other common prepositions:

about	above	after	among	around
at	before	below	beside	between
but	by	concerning	during	except
for	from	in	into	like
of	off	on	over	to
through	toward	under	until	up
upon	with	without		

Practice A. Write any appropriate preposition before each noun or pronoun. Check with your teacher when you are finished.

1._____ a restaurant   6._____ school
2._____ plane   7._____ train
3._____ six o'clock   8. _____ the field
4._____ his eyes   9._____ them
5._____ two chairs   10._____two people

53

How many prepositions can you spot in the following photographs? Write them all down.

Optional Practice. Discuss the photographs.
1. What activities are taking place?
2. How many nouns do you find?
3. How many adjectives do you see?

4. Which of these activities take place in your country too?
5. Do you participate in any of them?

Business English and Conversation - Armando Aceituno M.

Practice B. Complete these sentences with the appropriate preposition from the parenthesis.

1. This matter is_____her and me. (between, among)
2. Many people left _____ the plane. (on, by)
3. She's walking _____ school (for, to)
4. The glass is dirty. You can't see _____ it. (to, through)
5. The papers are on the shelf _____ your desk. (beside, in)
6. Put the documents _____ an envelope. (on, in)
7. Black is the opposite _____ white. (from, of)
8. She's explaining the case _____ them. (to, at)
9. Are you listening _____ me? (at, to)
10. He loves traveling _____ train. (by, on)

Practice C. Look at the following photograph and write three sentences based on it. Use as many prepositions as possible. Example:

The woman **with** glasses is holding a baby **in** her hands.

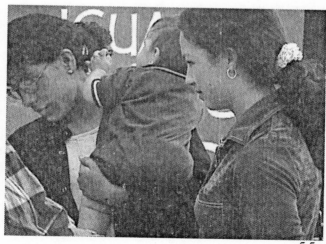

55

Practice D. Write any appropriate preposition before each noun or pronoun. Check with your teacher when you are finished.

1. _____ home   6. _____ the table
2. _____ work   7. _____ a mailbox
3. _____ the bus   8. _____ lunch
4. _____ her   9. _____ the bed
5. _____ two trees   10. _____ the tree

Practice E. Many times we make mistakes in the use of prepositions. Notice the special situations surrounding these examples.

1. The boy is inside the house. (NOT inside of)

2. He works outside the office. (NOT outside of)

3. She walked into the room. (NOT in) [1]

4. They looked in the cabinet. (NOT into)

5. The box is beside the shelf. (NOT besides) [2]

6. In regard to this project... (NOT in regard with)

7. In regard to your loan... (NOT in regards to)

8. Where did he go? (NOT where did he go to?)

9. Where is she? (NOT where is she at?)

10. All of them are here. (NOT all them)

11. Both of us are working. (NOT both us)

12. All the boys are late. (NOT All of the boys)

13. Both the girls study hard. (NOT both of the girls) [3]

14. I agree to the rules. (Agree to rules, procedures, etc.)

15. I agree with Mr. Taylor (Agree with people)

[1] INTO when you are talking about movement. IN talks about position. IN THE ROOM would be correct if you were walking inside the room.
[2] BESIDE means next to. BESIDES means in addition to.
[3] Use OF before a pronoun. Omit OF before a noun.

Practice F. The following sentences illustrate the incorrect use of prepositions. Correct them.

1. Where are the books at?

_____

2. Both of the cars were destroyed.

_____

3. I can never agree to Julie.

_____

4. We are writing in regards to your letter.

_____

5. Our family is inside of the house.

_____

6. All of the desks need to be repaired.

_____

7. Put the tank besides the couch.

_____

8. Their car is parked outside of the garage.

_____

9. Where is he going to?

_____

10. He divided the money between Carol, Eva, and me.

_____

11. Share your knowledge with both them.

_____

12. Did you look into the drawer?

_____

Conjunctions

 Conjunctions connect words or groups of words. They can be coordinate, correlative or subordinate.

Some **coordinate conjunctions:**

and	but	for	or
so	yet	nor	

Sample sentences:

She doesn't like you **nor** me.
He eats chocolate **and** ice cream.
They wanted to pass the exam, **but** she didn't study.

Correlative conjunctions : (they are used in pairs)

both...and	neither...nor
not only...but also	either...or

Sample sentences:

Neither Nancy **nor** Karla understood the problem.
Both Michelle **and** Lilian failed Shorthand.
Not only Robert **but also** Michael came to say hello.

Subordinate conjunctions:

after	when	unless	although	though
until	as	before	as if	since
where	that	as though	because	whether
while	if	provided	(and others)	

Sample sentences:

William sold the horse **because** it was sick.
He talked about the book **as though** he had read it.
She won't listen to me **unless** you tell her the truth.

Practice A. Complete the following sentences with <u>any</u> appropriate conjunction. Some spaces may have more than one possible answer.

1. She got the folder _____ put it on my desk.
2. He looked for the horse, _____ he didn't see it.
3. Eat that hamburger _____ it looks delicious.
4. Frank _____ Joseph made the deal.
5. I'd like to take you to the movies, _____ I don't have money.

Optional Reading and Writing Practice – Read the completed sentences from Practice A in silence, then paraphrase them in your notebook.

Practice B. Orally or in writing, make complete sentences using the conjunctions in parenthesis.
1. (unless) _____
2. (as though) _____
3. (neither...nor) _____
4. (until) _____
5. (since) _____
6. (yet) _____
7. (nor) _____
8. (both..and) _____
9. (whether) _____
10. (while)_____

Interjections

We use interjections to express strong feelings or emotions. They are usually followed by an exclamation point.

Some examples:

Shoot!	No!	Wow!	Great!
My God!	Darn!	Hurray!	Hey!

Practice A. Write a sentence after each of the following interjections.

1. Great!_____

2. My God! _____

3. Wow! _____

4. Oh, no!_____

5. Hurray!_____

Practice B. <u>Underline</u> the conjunctions in the following sentences.

1. Not only Ralph but also Emily came to our party.

2. George didn't go because it was too far away.

3. I tried to tell him the truth, but it was too late.

4. Either use your fountain pen or put it away.

5. She asked the same thing as though she didn't know.

6. I told him to come later since it was too early.

7. Both Janice and Dony are here.

8. He's bought many sweaters, yet he can't find one.

9. Christie wanted to eat spaghetti and meatballs.

10. Neither Ingrid nor Yvette enjoyed the show.

Optional Writing Practice – In your notebook, write five sentences using conjunctions.

Optional Conversation Practice – Explain to your classmates what the following terms mean: budget, meat, transaction, far away, put away, party, hurray.

Showing Possession

Possession can be shown in English with nouns, pronouns, or adjectives.

With nouns:
This is the car of Joanne.
This is <u>Joanne's car</u>.
I found the notebook of Mary.
I found Mary's notebook.

For this we use an apostrophe and S ('s) before the noun.

Mr. Wilson's book
The children's toys

If the noun is a plural form that ends with "s", add only the apostrophe.

The books of the boys-   The <u>boys' books</u>

With possessive adjectives:

my	**its**	**your**	**our**	**his**	**her**	**their**

The car of Joanne	-	**Her** car
The cars of the people	-	**Their** cars
The sons of Michelle	-	**Her** sons
The life of Paul	-	**His** life

61

With possessive pronouns.

mine   its   yours   ours his   hers theirs

> This pen is mine.   That bus is yours.
> The problem is his.   The books are theirs.

Practice A. Change the following long forms to the short forms.

0. The car of Joanne.   0. <u>Joanne's car</u>.

1. The cat of Michael   _____
2. The hat of James   _____
3. The TV of my mother   _____
4. The radio of my sister _____
5. The dresses of those girls _____
6. The skirts of your nephew _____
7. The vest of my niece _____
8. The helmet of her boyfriend _____
9. The binoculars of Tom _____
10. The sunglasses of Victor _____

Practice B. Write the possessive form using a possessive adjective.

0. The face of the man   <u>**His face**</u>

1. The job of the woman _____
2. The end of the line _____
3. The orbits of the planets _____
4. The home of my friends_____
5. The new car of William_____
6. The friend of Amy _____
7. The symbols of the clubs _____
8. The eyes of Evelyn _____
9. The nose of Melissa _____
10. The heart of Oscar _____

General Practice and Review

A. Write the plural form of the following nouns.

1. moose _____
2. board _____
3. duty _____
4. mouse _____
5. sheep _____

6. ash_____
7. wife_____
8. boy_____
9. chief_____
10. house_____

B. Underline the adverbs in the following sentences.

1. Here comes your new car!
2. It is well built and extremely cheap.
3. Do you really like it very much?
4. You can always take it with you.
5. I will see you later.

C. Write the comparative and superlative forms of each adjective.

POSITIVE	COMPARATIVE	SUPERLATIVE
1. large	_____	_____
2. good	_____	_____
3. silly	_____	_____
4. ridiculous	_____	_____
5. bad	_____	_____
6. wide	_____	_____
7. reliable	_____	_____
8. strange	_____	_____
9. long	_____	_____
10. interesting	_____	_____

D. Write the plural form of the following nouns.

1. leaf _____   6. child_____
2. hero_____   7. gentleman_____
3. louse_____   8. lunch_____
4. foot_____   9. fairy_____
5. goose_____   10. diary_____

E. Underline all the pronouns used in the following sentences.

1. They never found him.
2. Where are they now?
3. Wendy told me to get lost.
4. When we find it, leave.
5. I never understood.

F. Complete the following sentences with the correct pronoun or adjective from the parenthesis.

1. I found your passbook, but not_____ . (my, mine)
2. _____ deductions are wrong. (Your, Yours)
3. Did you see _____ hair? (her, hers)
4. We'll work with his computer or with_____. (her, hers)
5. When_____ grades are here, I'll check them. (our, ours)
6. Ralph took _____ suits to the laundry. (our, ours)
7. She never found _____ skates. (her, hers)
8. Yes, _____ remembers me. (her, she)
9. _____ story was incredible. (My, Mine)
10. _____ moms have been hired. (Their, Theirs)

G. Complete the following sentences using the comparative or superlative form of the adjective in parenthesis.

1. I finally got a _____ dog. (large)
2. Isn't your job _____ than mine? (tiring)
3. This show is _____ of all. (boring)
4. Pat is _____ than Joe. (considerate)
5. Movies are _____ this year than last. (scary)
6. She's the _____ of the two. (pretty)
7. We are much _____ than you. (fast)
8. They look _____. (intelligent)
9. My boat was _____. (expensive)
10. But his was _____. (modern)

With your classmates, play STOP. The teacher will tell you a letter, for example: P. You must then write as many nouns and adjectives with that letter as you can in 30 seconds. When the time has expired, the teacher will say "Stop!" and the one with the most words is the winner.

Adjectives	Nouns

🗣 Conversation Tidbits ✓

①

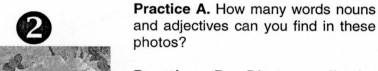

②

Practice A. How many words nouns and adjectives can you find in these photos?

Practice B. Discuss all the photographs. What feelings do they arouse in you? Are they inspiring in any way? If so, why?

③

Business English and Conversation   -   Armando Aceituno M.

Chapter 4 — Verbs

Verbs are the all-essential words in any language, just like nouns. Without them, no one anywhere can do anything.

Verbs can express physical or mental actions, or situations:

She runs...   He has...
I am...   We want...
He is...   Christy smiles...

Verbs can be Action or Linking, Regular or Irregular, Transitive or Intransitive. But before we get into that, we must see about a rule which troubles many students of English as a Foreign or Second Language.

S or ES?

Adding "S" or "ES" to the verb in the present tense.

It is extremely important to keep these spelling rules for verbs when the subject is third person singular (he, she, it).

◈ **Add only "s" to most verbs.**

I see   she **sees**   we keep   he **keeps**
They take   Pablo **takes**   You follow   Mary **follows**

◈ **Add "es" if the verb ends in "s", "x", "ch", "sh", "z", or "o".**

mix   **mixes**   go   **goes**
catch   **catches**   buzz   **buzzes**

❖ **When the verb ends in "y" preceded by a consonant, then change that "y" into "i", before adding "es".**

    try   <u>tries</u>   cry   <u>cries</u>

❖ **"Be" and "Have" are exceptions**, since they have their own forms for HE, SHE and IT.

<u>**BE**</u>   <u>**HAVE**</u>
She <u>is</u>   She <u>has</u>
David<u>is</u>   David <u>has</u>

Practice A. Add "s" or "es" to the following verbs.

1. cook_____
2. write_____
3. undo_____
4. run_____
5. play_____
6. caress_____
7. drive_____
8. file_____

9. bug_____
10. push_____
11. pull_____
12. plant_____
13. forego_____
14. bother_____
15. insist_____

Practice B. Look up in your dictionary as many synonyms and antonyms as possible for the following verbs.

undo	caress	bug
pull	forego	bother
insist	try	cry
decide	compose	create
want	activate	deride
smite	befall	arouse
excite	adapt	connect

As we had previously stated, verbs can be Action or Linking, Regular or Irregular, Transitive or Intransitive.

An **action verb** expresses movement, activities, thoughts or ideas.

<u>Movement</u>	<u>Thoughts</u>	<u>Activities</u>
run	think	read
walk	decide	create
jump	want	sleep
go	wish	dream
come	love	compose

A **linking verb** connects the subject to the rest of the sentence.

Some common linking verbs:

is	look*
am	smell*
are	feel*
was	sound*
were	taste*

* These verbs can be used as linking or action.

Examples of sentences with linking verbs:

This material **feels** soft.
    That idea **sounds** great.
        She **seems** sad.
            Peter **is** very quiet today.
            Christian **is** very active.
                We **were** students last year.

Regular vs. Irregular verbs

The difference between regular and irregular verbs is mostly the way they form their past and past participle forms.

To change regular verbs into their past and past participle forms we add "ed" to their base form in one of the following ways.

1. Just add "d" or "ed".

dissolve	dissolved	bake	baked
state	stated	chew	chewed
bother	bothered	call	called
smell	smelled	taste	tasted

2. If the final "y" is preceded by a consonant, change it into "i" before adding "ed".

try	tried	fry	fried
employ	employed	play	played

3. If the final consonant is preceded by a single vowel, double it. (Verbs of only one syllable)

step	stepped	nod	nodded

4. If the final consonant is preceded by a single vowel, and the accent is on the last syllable, double it. (Verbs of two syllables or more)

defer	deferred	prefer preferred

Exception: acquit   acquitted

Irregular verbs do not always follow specific rules to change into their past and past participle forms.

Examples of Irregular Verbs:

BASE FORM	PAST FORM	PAST PARTICIPLE FORM
be	was, were	been
eat	ate	eaten
drink	drank	drunk
bring	brought	brought
cut	cut	cut
fly	flew	flown
put	put	put
do	did	done
smite	smote	smitten
read	read	read

Practice A. Write the past and past participle forms of the following verbs. Consult your dictionary if necessary.

BASE FORM	PAST FORM	PAST PARTICIPLE
1. be	_____	_____
2. freeze	_____	_____
3. choose	_____	_____
4. give	_____	_____
5. write	_____	_____
6. go	_____	_____
7. see	_____	_____
8. know	_____	_____
9. shake	_____	_____
10. speak	_____	_____

Transitive vs. Intransitive

Transitive verbs have a direct object that receives the action in the sentence.

> 1. They finished <u>their homework</u> quickly.
> 2. She looked at <u>the door.</u>
> 3. They took <u>the bus.</u>
> 4. He wrote <u>a long letter.</u>

To understand the concept of direct object, it is necessary to ask what or who receives the action of the verb. Look back at the previous sentences.

> 1. What did they finish?
> 2. What did she look at?
> 3. What did they take?
> 4. What did he write?

Practice A. Underline the direct object in each sentence.

> 1. Victor doesn't forget his horrible experience.
>
> 2. His aunt sent a large package.
>
> 3. Jennie didn't understand that exercise.
>
> 4. Your niece got a new car.
>
> 5. Bill wrote a nice book.
>
> 6. My nephew didn't find his gold watch.
>
> 7. Barbara is listening to the radio at home.
>
> 8. The accountant doesn't have my statements.
>
> 9. Michael requested a new catalog.
>
> 10. Christina purchased a fur coat in that store.

Optional Reading and Writing Practice – Read the first five sentences from Practice A in silence, then paraphrase them in your notebook.

Intransitive verbs are those which don't need a direct object in the sentence.

He runs. She feels well.
They are angry. We were sick.

Linking verbs are <u>always</u> intransitive, but some verbs can be transitive or intransitive, depending on the meaning of the sentence.

He <u>runs</u> this company. (transitive)
He <u>runs</u> in the park. (intransitive)
She <u>sounds</u> the alarm. (transitive)
She <u>sounds</u> angry! (intransitive)
I <u>taste</u> the ribs. (transitive)
The ribs <u>taste</u> great. (intransitive)

Practice B. Underline only the intransitive verbs.

1. Carol doesn't work well.
2. Rick runs faster than Bob.
3. The programmer forgot his glasses.
4. Barbara took my books.
5. Iris and George came here yesterday.
6. Your doctor didn't bring his pen.
7. Karen failed English again.
8. Hector wants a red bike.
9. Does your son have a pet?
10. Nancy and Julie don't understand French.

Optional Conversation Practice
Explain to your classmates the difference between Transitive and Intransitive verbs.

Practice C. Underline the direct object in each sentence.

1. My doctor prescribed some medicine.
2. Some students don't want the new rules.
3. Alice uses the telephone in the mornings.
4. Your lawyer lost the case.
5. The secretary didn't file all the documents.

Practice D. Form the past tense of the following regular verbs.

BASE FORM	PAST TENSE	BASE FORM	PAST TENSE
1. agree_____		6. touch_____	
2. enjoy_____		7. beg _____	
3. dry _____		8. clean_____	
4. look _____		9. walk_____	
5. bake_____		10. prefer _____	

Practice E. Answer the following questions:
1. What is a verb?
2. What is a regular verb?
3. What is a linking verb?
4. What is a transitive verb?

Optional Pronunciation and Spelling Practide. Read aloud and spell the following verbs and nouns.

agree	disagree	pedigree
prefer	refer	defer
prescribe	describe	transcribe
preclude	include	seclude
mislead	misinterpret	misunderstand
flog	clog	unclog

Auxiliary Verbs

Do, does, did   Could   May   Can
Have, has, had   Might   Shall   Must
To be   Will   Should   Ought to

These auxiliary verbs function in a different way from normal verbs:

1. They are used with the base form of the main verb.

will see   can have   must talk to

Except TO BE and HAVE...

is looking   have been   are doing   has become

2. Interrogative sentences begin with the auxiliary verb.

> **Shall** I send you my résumé?
> **Can** you move that shelf by yourself?

3. Do not use two of them together, except HAVE as in "must have been", "should have seen", etc.

Their approximate meanings are the following:
WILL and SHALL express future, determination.
WOULD is normally considered the past tense of Will, and it is also used in conditions.
CAN expresses ability, capacity, to have the power.
MAY expresses possibility, uncertainty, permission.
COULD expresses ability, capacity, probability.
MIGHT expresses probability, uncertainty.
SHOULD and OUGHT TO express obligation, necessity
MUST expresses obligation, necessity.

Using auxiliaries, write as many sentences as possible about these photographs.

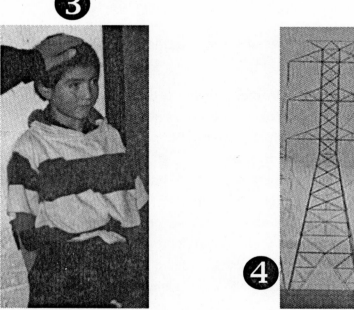

Business English and Conversation - Armando Aceituno M.

Problem Verbs

Some verbs can be confusing as far as their usage is concerned. The following guidelines will help you overcome some common obstacles which students of EFL and ESL face.

Say and Tell Use Say when you are speaking in general, not necessarily to a particular person.

> She says (that) the wind is blowing strong.
> He says (that) he will never come back.
> They say it's time to go.
> She said she was going home.

SAY is intransitive, it does not need an object. TELL, on the other hand, is transitive; it must have an object.

> She tells us when to begin.
> I told them to leave.
> They told me it was time to go.
> He told me he was going home.

Practice A. Use the appropriate form of TELL or SAY from the parenthesis.

1. We _____ him to stay here. (told, said)

2. She _____ that her mother is prettier. (tells, says)

3. They _____ us where to go. (will tell, will say)

4. Daniel _____ he is tired. (tells, says)

5. Bob _____ them where the map was. (told, said)

6. I _____ her to buy the carnations. (told, said)

7. She _____ she can drive. (tells, says)

8. They _____ that we were crazy. (told, said)

9. I _____ my sister to come. (told, said)

10. She _____ me that she would come. (told, said)

Borrow and Lend

These are opposite verbs. To borrow means to receive from someone, and to lend means to give.

Examples:

She borrowed our pens. (She received)
We lent our pencils to her. (We gave)
I borrowed her book. (I obtained)
She lent me her book. (She gave)

Earn and Win

Both these verbs give the idea of receiving something.

YOU WIN

a race
a competition
a contest
an election
points in a game

YOU EARN

a salary
recognition
points in an exam
interest on your investments

But, you don't win a class or an exam; you <u>pass</u> a class and an exam.

Remember and Remind

Use "remember" when you are thinking of something, someone, a memory, etc. To remember means to reminisce. Use "remind" to tell someone about something important.

EXAMPLES:
I remember our last meeting.
She remembers my birthday.
Remember to buy the groceries.
Did you remember your wedding anniversary?

I reminded him about the meeting.
She reminds me of my grandmother.
Remind me to buy the groceries
Did she remind you of your wedding anniversary?

Practice B. Choose the correct word from the parenthesis to complete the sentences.

1. Benjamin _____ the Boston Marathon. (earned, won)

2. I _____ him to work here. (said, told)

3. We _____ that we didn't have it. (said, told)

4. Michelle_____ him her address book. (borrowed, lent)

5. Did you _____ money from Hector? (borrow, lend)

6. They _____ that they are faster. (say, tell)

7. Lindsay _____ her cousin to get up early. (remembered, reminded)

8. The boss _____ our first sale. (remembers, remind)

9. She _____ me her typewriter. (lent, borrowed)

10. Wendy _____ me to go to the doctor. (said, told)

Use **HOPE** when you desire or wish something.

Use **WAIT** when you are physically and actually waiting for someone or something to arrive or occur.

Use **EXPECT** when you have the certainty that something is going to happen.

I hope I get good grades this year.
He hopes his business be better now.
I hope I understand the question.

They told me to wait for them.
Please wait for my cousin. She'll be here soon.
She's waiting for her husband. He's late.

I expect to pass this course. I studied hard.
He won't like the news. I expect him to be mad.

These verbs also have very definite meanings.

DO	MAKE
homework	objects (manufacture)
duties or chores	time (while waiting)
tasks	up your mind (decide)
assignments	up with someone (reconcile differences)

 Get means to obtain, Take means to grab or receive. Both verbs have their meanings changed through the use of prepositions or other words.

SOME EXAMPLES:

	along (to advance, be in harmony with)
	around (travel, circumvent)
	away with (escape)
	up (sit up or stand)
	something (grab, obtain)
GET	on (board a vehicle - public transportation)
	going (start, begin a trip, walk, job, etc.)
	on with it (continue)
	off (exit vehicle - public transportation)
	by (pass, succeed)

	off (remove)
	down (destroy, undo)
	away (remove, seize, steal)
TAKE	back (recover)
	care (guard, watch over)
	charge (control)
	after (look or be like someone else)
	apart (destroy, dismantle)

Business English and Conversation - Armando Aceituno M.

Practice C. Complete the sentences with the correct word from the parenthesis.

1. Susan _____ her wish. (took, got)
2. John _____ to graduate this year. (hopes, waits)
3. Why did she _____ pancakes? (do, make)
4. Verito didn't _____ her homework. (do, make)
5. Victor _____ off at the next bus stop. (takes, gets)
6. When does he _____ his cousin? (expect, wait)
7. Wendy is _____ for us. (expecting, waiting)
8. Daniel must be _____ us. (expecting, waiting)
9. Where do you _____ for your ride? (expect, wait)
10. Julie was lucky in _____ the job. (getting, waiting)

 Conversation Tidbits ✓

There are at least ten verbs in this photograph. How many can you find?
How many adjectives?
How many nouns

Common Mistakes

English is a very extensive language. It has a huge vocabulary which, some experts say, contains more than 500,000 words, including declensions, inflections, conjugations, etc. It has a well defined grammatical structure (with about ten zillion exceptions), and much more. It is not altogether rare, therefore, to make mistakes sometimes while speaking or writing in English.

There are some scholars somewhere who have achieved an exceptional mastery of the language, but the rest of us mortals must console ourselves in our ignorance and do our best to try to use the language well.

This section presents some common mistakes which are committed in the regular usage of English (Yes, even by native speakers).

Problems with Pronouns

Don't be afraid. It's only me!
Everybody knows their own business.
She's the candidate who I like the most.

Do these sentences sound familiar? Yes, they are normal, everyday expressions and statements which people tend to use. Yes, they are all incorrect.

Using pronouns correctly is as important in English as it is in many other languages. Yet, there are many mistakes which people make and that are generally accepted by most as part of our normal language.
To use pronouns correctly we need to know about Case, Reference and Antecedent.

CASE: Personal pronouns have these cases: Subjective, Objective, and Possessive. We'll worry mostly about the first two.

SUBJECTIVE	OBJECTIVE
I	me
you	you
he	him
she	her
it	it
they	them
we	us
who	whom
whoever	whomever

1. The Subjective case is used as the subject in the sentences. It should be doing the action, not receiving it.

> She handled it very well, didn't she?
> It was I who brought the leaflets.

2. The Objective case is used only as an object. It can never be executing an action; it always receives it.

> I told him to be quiet.
> The matter is only between you and me.
> Send them their receipt as soon as possible.

REFERENCE: This matter is somewhat more complicated but still easy to understand. It simply means that the pronoun must agree with the noun it refers to (its antecedent). Look at the examples:

> David told Mike that he had weird hair.
> George told Erick that he had very nice teeth.

In the first sentence, who had weird hair? It may seem obvious to some that it was Mike, but if you read it more carefully, you will notice that the pronoun HE could also refer to David. In the second example we have the same problem. Who had the nice teeth?

To avoid this type of error, you may need to rewrite the whole sentence. For example:

David told Mike, "You have weird hair."

ANTECEDENT : Mike   **PRONOUN** : You

In the following examples you will see the pronouns underlined and the antecedents in bold letters.

> **Bob** hasn't made as much money as <u>he</u> had hoped.
> **Daniel and Victor** don't perform the way <u>they</u> could.
> Take **this car** and sell <u>it</u>.
> **Mariela** says that Ann will wait for <u>her</u> until Monday.

Nonexistent words and contractions

1. AIN'T : In colloquial English, this has the meaning of ISN'T, AREN'T, AM NOT, HASN'T, and HAVEN'T. In your correspondence and other documents, avoid using it at all costs.

2. GONNA and WANNA are normally accepted in conversation, but, by all means, do not use them in written communication. Use their spellings: GOING TO and WANT TO.

3. IF I WOULD'VE... This should be: IF I HAD... : "If I had been there, I would've seen it." WOULD'VE is quite correct when used to show the result, not the condition.

4. WOULD OF, COULD OF, SHOULD OF, etc. Since the contraction "VE", as in could have = **could've**, sounds similar to the word "OF", some people have started using the preposition "OF" instead of the real contraction 'VE.

Language Interference

Sometimes we try to say something in English after translating it from another language. This gives as a result sentences such as these:

It doesn't like me.   *(From Spanish structure)*
I before worked here.   *(From Chinese structure)*

What we were trying to say:

I don't like it.
I used to work here.

How can we avoid language interference? THINK in English. This may seem difficult at first, but it becomes easier with PRACTICE, a lot of practice. That's the reason you should...

Practice in class by participating as much as possible.
Practice after class. There are many ways of doing this:

With your classmates and friends.
By forming a club with other students.

Practice by yourself all the time. Force yourself to think always in English. It will be hard at first, but if you keep doing it, you will soon find yourself thinking in English with no problem.

One of the most common excuses for not using spoken English is "Someone may laugh at me if I don't say it right". But it is a proven fact that if you want to improve your English, you cannot worry about what others might say or think. You have to think of what is best for you and do whatever is necessary to achieve your ultimate objective in studying another language: fluency.

Incorrect use of plurals and/or verbs

As silly as it may seem, you must remember that in English the following rules apply:

1. People refers to more than one. It is a plural noun which cannot be used in a singular form.

correct:	People are crazy.
incorrect:	People is crazy.
correct:	People have strange views.
incorrect:	People has strange views.

2. News is a noun which does not have a plural form. Hence:

correct:	The news is good.
incorrect:	The news are good.

3. The prefixes EVERY, SOME, ANY, and NO (everybody, someone, anybody, nothing, etc.), refer to a third person singular. This means that the main verb we use must agree with the subject if it is one of the above.

	Everybody should bring his chair.
NOT	Everybody should bring their chairs.

	Everything seems normal.
NOT	Everything seem normal.

	Anybody who comes late is a fool.
NOT	Anybody who comes late are fools.

	Everyone knows his or her place.
NOT	Everyone knows their place.

	Everybody has his or her time.
NOT	Everyone has their time.

Business English and Conversation - Armando Aceituno M.

Had Better

Had Better expresses a strong warning, stronger than SHOULD and very similar to MUST. (See **Auxiliaries** in the next section) The phrase is acceptable, as long as the *had* or its contraction is preserved:

> You had better do it or You'd better do it
>
> **NOT**   You better do it

AFFIRMATIVE
> You'd better study if you want to pass the exam.
> Marianne had better go back now.
> We'd better get a larger car.
> You'd better tell him the truth.
> She'd better buy more beans.

NEGATIVE
> We'd better not show him the results.
> He'd better not give them the money.
> You'd better not come late.
> She'd better not get up late.
> John had better not be inside.

INTERROGATIVE
> Hadn't you better leave now?
> Hadn't she better work by herself?
> Hadn't we better go?
> Hadn't David better take this?
> Hadn't you better study?

Notice that interrogative sentences with Had Better are always in the negative form. (hadn't)

Optional Conversation Practice. Explain to your classmates the meaning of HAD BETTER. Use the phrase in three different sentences.

USES OF "IT" AND "ING"

A. The pronoun "IT" can be used as a subject when we talk about the weather, days, seasons, or an action in general.

It's raining right now.   I's sunny today.
Thank God it's Friday!   Boy! It's really windy out there.
It's cold in Alaska, isn't it?   It's finally summer!
It's hard to be humble.   It's good to see you again.

Remember: a sentence MUST NOT begin with Is or Are unless it is a question.

Wrong: Is easy to swim.
Right: It's easy to swim.

> **Wrong**: Is nice to know you're loved.
> **Right**: It's nice to know you're loved.

> **Wrong**: Are the most expensive these.
> **Right**: These are the most expensive.

> **Wrong**: Is snowing.
> **Right**: It's snowing.

Practice 1. Complete each sentence with the appropriate word or words from the parenthesis.

1. _____ good to see you. (It's, Is)
2. _____ nice to be back. (It's, Is)
3. _____ the circus in town? (It's, Is)
4. _____ a difficult exam. (It's, Is)
5. _____ time to get up. (It's, Is)
6. Get up before _____ too late. (it's, is)
7. Do you know what time _____? (it is, is)
8. _____ talking about you. (Are, They are)
9. _____ the students mad? (Are, They are)
10. _____ a miracle! (It's, is)

B. The "ING" form can also be used in different ways.

a. As a **verb** following the verb To Be: (progressive tenses)
> She is listening to the radio.
> We were thinking of you.

b. As a **noun**:
> Listening to the radio relaxes me.
> Reading makes me sleepy.
> Playing chess is not difficult.

c. As an **adjective**:
> Crying babies make me nervous.
> The sleeping child looks lovely.
> Those dancing couples aren't tired.

 Adding "ing" to the verb

The following spelling rules are important to remember, because the "ING" form of the verb is used a lot in some of the tenses we are going to see in the next section of this book.

1. If the verb ends in a consonant preceded by a single vowel, double the consonant (one-syllable verbs):
> sto**pp**ing   be**gg**ing   qui**tt**ing

2. In verbs of more than one syllable, double the last consonant preceded by a single vowel, **if** the stress falls on the last syllable.
> prefe**rr**ing   refe**rr**ing
> > Exception: acqui**tt**ing

3. Change the "ie" ending into "y", then add "ing".
> lie - l**y**ing   die - d**y**ing   vie - v**y**ing

4. Drop the final "e" before adding ING if it is preceded by a consonant.
> write - writing   bake - baking
> agree - agreeing   see - seeing

5. All other verbs, just add "ing".

bringing ending crying

Practice A. Add "ing" to the following verbs.

1. like_____
2. try_____
3. tie_____
4. tag_____
5. travel_____

6. cancel_____
7. refer_____
8. do_____
9. double_____
10. clean_____

Write as many verbs (or sentences) as possible about these photographs. Use the ING form.

General Practice and Review

A. Write any appropriate adjective before each noun.

1. _____ accountant
2. _____ flowchart
3. _____ city
4. _____ people
5. _____ food

6. _____ oxen
7. _____ briefcase
8. _____ mice
9. _____ teeth
10. _____ sheet

B. Write the comparative form of each adjective.

POSITIVE COMPARATIVE POSITIVE COMPARATIVE

1. beautiful_____
2. honest_____
3. greedy_____
4. big _____
5. nice _____

6. smart_____
7. intelligent_____
8. young_____
9. pretty_____
10. darling_____

C. Add "s" or "es" to the following verbs, if necessary.

1. My sister do____
2. People want____
3. Churches collect____
4. Johanna purchase____
5. Your father say____

6. The dog chew____
7. His mother wash____
8. They go____
9. Dony like____
10. Our nephew fight____

D. Complete the following sentences with the correct pronoun or adjective from the parenthesis.

1. Have you seen _____ lamp? (my, mine)
2. Don't erase _____ file. (your, yours)
3. Hers is here, but I don't see _____. (my, mine)
4. I'd like to meet _____ nephew. (her, hers)
5. _____ is in the closet. (Ours, Our)
6. When did they get _____ grades? (theirs, their)
7. We don't understand _____ kids. (ours, our)
8. If your handwriting is bad, _____ is worse. (mine, my)
9. Talk to _____ teacher. (yours, your)
10. Reset _____ computer. (her, hers)
11. Alice found her purse, but not _____ . (your, yours)
12. They forgot _____ tapes. (theirs, their)
13. Where is _____ ? (my, mine)
14. _____ son is making her cry. (Their, Theirs)
15. Put your books next to _____ . (our, ours)

E. Write "T" (Transitive) or "I" (Intransitive) for each underlined verb.

1. _____ Jessica talks too fast.
2. _____ My car doesn't run.
3. _____ Where is Mark?
4. _____ Monica watched the show.
5. _____ Those dogs ate my lunch.
6. _____ Why am I here?
7. _____ Beatriz cooked dinner for us.
8. _____ Some cats are outside.
9. _____ Who broke the lamp?
10. _____ Hellen has a headache.
11. _____ Brian didn't lose his money.
12. _____ Does the computer function correctly?
13. _____ Karla doesn't like anybody.
14. _____ Daniel and I already washed our hands.
15. _____ Did his daughter see you?

Chapter 5

Other Structures Part I

Now that we have talked about the parts of speech, it is time to put them together to form sentences of all kinds. For this, we will take a brief look at affirmative, negative and interrogative sentences in the main tenses, as well as their structures:

Simple Present, Simple Past and Simple Future
> Rodney goes home after school.
> Rodney went home after school.
> Rodney will go home after school.

Present, Past and Future Progressive
> Rodney is going home.
> Rodney was going home.
> Rodney will be going home.

Present, Past and Future Perfect
> Rodney has gone home.
> Rodney had gone home.
> Rodney will have gone home.

Conditions and auxiliary verbs
> Rodney must go home.
> If Rodney could go home, he would.

It is not really necessary for you to memorize all the structures and tenses. Instead, it is more effective to learn them by actually putting them into practice. There are, however, some elements we must look at first.

For instance, here are some common contractions:

is not	**isn't**	are not	**aren't**
do not	**don't**	does not	**doesn't**
cannot	**can't**	should not	**shouldn't**

93

will not	**won't**	must not	**mustn't**
has not	**hasn't**	have not	**haven't**
could not	**couldn't**	would not	**wouldn't**
I have	**I've**	she has done	**she's** done
I would	**I'd**	I had gone	**I'd** gone
she would	**she'd**	she had been	**she'd** been
he would	**he'd**	he had seen	**he'd** seen

Recognition Practice. In the following reading, circle all the verbs in the past tense. Don't circle each more than once.

Tameless
by T. Bird

This is not the story of a man named Brady, nor William, nor John. Nope, his name was not a very usual name. That's because he was not even a man . That's right, he was a she. She was a girl, a nice, clean, quiet girl named Tameless.

You might say that Tameless does not even sound like a name, and you're right. But you see, Tameless was not a very usual girl and she did not live in a very usual place. Tameless lived in Stayless, a country located north of Nowhere. In Stayless, people had very unusual names. For example, Tameless' best friends were Matchless and Speechless. Yes, all the names ended in **less**. They had to, because that was the law of the land.

Tameless had two very ugly half-sisters, Dipless and Reckless, and an even uglier and evil step-mother, Hopeless. Actually, the only thing ugly about them was their eyebrows, but that was the sign of beauty in Stayless. If anyone had long, terse eyebrows, that person was considered beautiful. But if the eyebrows were wrinkled, then ugliness had definitely set in.

Hopeless was bitter because when she was young, she had been a beautiful woman, but as she grew older, (she was now 25, which in Stayless, it meant that she was an extremely old woman), her eyebrows started to wrinkle beyond recognition, her mood became more and more like that of a witch. She was so ugly now, that she had banished all mirrors from her house.

Tag Questions

Tag Questions, also called Tag Endings, are not even questions. They are expressions added to the end of a sentence to emphasize the statement or to verify that what we have said is true.

Examples: You are coming late today, **aren't you?**
He doesn't like bananas, **does he?**
She has a nice yacht, **doesn't she?**
Karl has broken the rules, **hasn't he?**
I am taller than he, **am I not?**

Although some scholars do not include tag questions as a grammatical item, there are some very definite rules:

1. If the sentence is affirmative, the tag question is usually negative and vice versa.

I am here, <u>am I not?</u>
Joe is angry, <u>isn't he?</u>
We got lost, <u>didn't we?</u>
She doesn't like apples, <u>does she?</u>
They wouldn't try, <u>would they?</u>

Notice that we usually use contractions in negative tag questions.

2. You must use the same auxiliary, verb to be, or Do-Does-Did, in that order, whichever is necessary.

They like the seal on the envelopes, <u>don't they?</u>
We have rights, <u>don't we?</u>
He announced the embargo, <u>didn't he?</u>
This is just a drill, <u>isn't it?</u>
The processes aren't new, <u>are they?</u>
We will make this sale, <u>won't we?</u>

3. Tag questions always use pronouns, even if the subject is a proper noun.

> Stanley isn't in the garage, is <u>he?</u>
> Ralph and George were upset, weren't <u>they?</u>
> Bobby didn't get a chance, did <u>he?</u>
> Jenniffer could get sick, couldn't <u>she?</u>

Practice A. Add an appropriate tag question to these sentences which contain the verb TO BE.

1. Arthur is safe, _____?

2. They are accountants, _____?

3. Irving isn't very tall, _____?

4. We aren't callous, _____?

5. Peter was working, _____?

6. The car was stolen, _____?

7. Emily wasn't sincere, _____?

8. They were cleaning the disk drive, _____?

9. Rick and I weren't lost, _____?

10. The office was closed, _____?

Practice B. Add a tag question to these sentences containing auxiliaries.

1. Brenda can help, _____?

2. They will see it, _____?

3. Karl must keep the books, _____?

4. He should move his car, _____?

5. Caesar would like it, _____?

6. You will come back, _____?

7. Debbie won't return the blouse, _____?

8. These people shouldn't be here, _____?

9. Gerald hasn't seen this movie, _____?

10. Bob and I can't be blamed for this, _____?

Practice C. Add a tag question using DO, DOES, DON'T, or DOESN'T.

1. Louis likes to increase prices, _____?
2. I have the right to remain silent, _____?
3. Bill provides a lot of help, _____?
4. We endorse his candidacy, _____?
5. Laura and Leslie check the output, _____?
6. You like walking bare-footed, _____?
7. Jimmy enjoys buying junk, _____?
8. They look like thieves, _____?
9. Herbert doesn't understand much, _____?
10. He doesn't spare a nickel, _____?
11. Mrs. Grau doesn't speak Chinese, _____?
12. They don't know how to delete files, _____?
13. Maurice doesn't have a briefcase, _____?
14. It doesn't look good, _____?
15. You don't drive, _____?

Practice D. Add a tag question using DID or DIDN'T.

1. George and Susie arrived later, _____?
2. I drove much faster, _____?
3. Hugo blamed it on you, _____?
4. We broke curfew, _____?
5. Charles met his neighbor, _____?
6. You didn't read the forecast, _____?
7. Paul didn't print it, _____?
8. They didn't use the labels, _____?
9. Beatrice didn't buy the suit, _____?
10. She didn't get the franchise, _____?

Embedded Questions

Embedded Questions are clauses "embedded in" or "attached to" sentences. These clauses usually begin with an interrogative word (what, who, where, etc.) and do not follow the same structure as a normal question.

Normal question : What do they want?

Possible answer with embedded question
    Correct: I don't know what they want.
    Incorrect::   I don't know what do they want.

Notice the possible answers to these questions:
    What are they saying?
        I can't understand what they are saying.
    Who are they?
        I don't know who they are.
    Why did they come?
        I'd like to know why they came.
    Who is that gorgeous girl?
        I don't know who that gorgeous girl is.
Incorrect:
    I can't understand what are they saying.
    I don't know who are they.
    I'd like to know why did they come.
    I don't know who is that gorgeous girl.

Practice A. Complete an embedded question after each interrogative word.

1. I don't know who _____

2. She wants to tell me where _____

3. Did he say why _____?

4. I wonder what _____

5. He told me who _____

Practice B. Underline the embedded questions in the following sentences. The first one has been done for you.

1. I wonder <u>who invented school.</u>
2. They never told us what fringe benefits we had.
3. I don't remember who was pushing the reset button.
4. I'd like to know where you work.
5. It'd be nice to find out what you were doing at noon.
6. Did he tell you what you were supposed to do?
7. Do you know what your gross profits were last year?
8. Did she say when we had to save her programs?
9. She doesn't understand why she has to quit.
10. You didn't tell me who your guarantor is for this loan.
11. I can show you who is running things around here.
12. She will tell you where you can find me.
13. Does she know what she should wear to the party?
14. When will they announce who won the prize?
15. My wife wants to know who the manager is.

Answer and/or discuss with your teacher and classmates the following questions.

1. What is a tag question? (Give two examples)
2. What is an embedded question?
3. Do embedded questions exist in your native language?
4. Some languages do not have tag questions. Do they exist in your native language?

Active Voice And Passive Voice

These are two different ways of expressing the same thing.

In the active voice, the subject of the sentence performs the action.

Examples: Charles broke the rules.
                    Who broke the rules?   Charles
                  Xiomara found the jewels.
                    Who found the jewels? Xiomara

In the passive voice, the subject receives the action.

              The rule was broken.
                  What was broken?   The rule

The subject of this sentence, the rule, did not perform the action. Instead, it received the action.

Notice the difference between active and passive voice:

ACTIVE : Our company purchased a mainframe yesterday.
PASSIVE: A mainframe was purchased yesterday.

ACTIVE : Charles received an award.
PASSIVE: An award was received by Charles.

The passive voice uses the verb to be and the past participle of the main verb. Sometimes, we need to include the "doer" of the action at the end of the sentence.

              Many letters were written by Mark Twain.
              The jewels were taken by him.

Notice the above examples in the active voice:

              Mark Twain wrote many letters.
              He took the jewels.

Business English and Conversation - Armando Aceituno M.

Practice A. Orally or in writing, change the following sentences to the passive voice. Keep all sentences in the simple past tense. Follow the example.

Example

0. Everybody misunderstood the question.
   The question was misunderstood by everybody.
OR: **The question was misunderstood.**

1. I gave the reply.
2. We overwrote several sentences.
3. You made it brief.
4. Martha sent the fax.
5. He discovered the evidence.
6. They stole some new cars last week.
7. She gave us her real name.
8. Mark told them a true story.
9. It destroyed my confidence.
10. Susan produced the missing documents.

Practice B. Orally or in writing, change the following sentences from active to passive voice. Keep them in the same tense (present perfect).

Example   **0.** Rod has written a book.
            A book has been written by Rod.
OR: **A book has been written.**

1. My physician has prescribed some medicine.
2. The Committee has turned down the request.
3. Your attorney has filed the papers.
4. They have forgotten a promise.
5. The police officer has fired several shots.
6. We have maintained our high standards.
7. That fireman has put out the fire.
8. It has erased our records.
9. She has enjoyed the performance.
10. My secretary has forgotten my appointments.

Conditions With If

Read the following sentences:

• If I was in Chicago, I'd be enjoying myself.
• If he would've told me, I would've listened to him.
• She wouldn't be begging for help if she had took my advice.

These are all common conditions with IF. Yes, they are all wrong.

They contain some of the common mistakes people make when speaking or writing English. They ignore the fundamental rules for making or expressing a condition with IF.

Each statement has two parts: **the condition** and **the result**

CONDITION	RESULT
If I see him,	I'll tell him about the meeting.

The condition is the part which contains "IF". It can be the first or last part of the statement.

> If he discovers the gold, he'll be exuberant.
> He'll be exuberant if he discovers the gold.

Notice that when the condition is at the beginning, it is separated from the result by a comma. When the condition is at the end, the comma is omitted.

Examples: If she likes it, I'll buy it for her.
I'll buy it for her if she likes it.

There are three main types of conditions:

- Future
- Present
- Past unreal

1. **Future condition.** This statement expresses an action that begins in the present and ends in the future.

Examples:

> If we drop this radio, we'll break it.
> We'll break this radio if we drop it.
> If our holding company agrees, we'll make an offer.
> We'll make an offer if our holding company agrees.

2. **Past condition.** This statement begins in the past and ends in a "conditional present" with could, would, etc. *Notice the change from the previous structure.*

> If we dropped this radio, we would break it.
> We would break this radio if we dropped it.
> If our holding company agreed, we'd make an offer.
> We'd make an offer if our holding company agreed.
> If the spreadsheet were full, we'd open a new one.
> We'd open a new spreadsheet if this one were full.
> If she waited a while, she would see him.
> She would see him if she waited a while

3. **Past Unreal** (Also called Past Impossible). This type of condition expresses an action that didn't happen. It can sometimes be like expressing a desire, wishing it had happened.

Examples:

> We didn't drop this radio, but if we had dropped it, we would have broken it.
> We would have broken this radio if we had dropped it.

The condition is in the past perfect (auxiliary HAD + Past Participle), and the result uses WOULD HAVE, COULD HAVE, etc. + the past participle. We can also use the contractions COULD'VE, WOULD'VE, etc. Look at the other examples on the following page.

a. We didn't make the offer because our holding company didn't agree.

If our holding company had agreed, we would have made an offer.

We would've made an offer if our holding company had agreed.

b. We didn't open a new spreadsheet because the first one wasn't full.

If the spreadsheet had been full, we would've opened a new one.

We would've opened a new spreadsheet if the first one had been full.

There are exceptions to the preceding rules. For example:

1. When we are stating an action or fact which is always true.

If mother sees our room dirty, she gets mad.

I'm always careful if I'm home alone.

Here, IF has the equivalent meaning of WHEN.

2. In imperative clauses.

If you see the mirror, take it.

If you find the gold watch, take care of it.

Practice A. Orally or in your notebook, make a condition (past unreal) based on the following statements.

1. Maurice didn't talk to his wife because she wasn't here.

1. If his wife had been here, Maurice would've talked to her.

2. We didn't inherit that money because the deceased didn't know us.

3. Lilian didn't insert the word because I didn't tell her.

4. I didn't store the wheels because the garage wasn't open.

5. Leslie didn't meet the requirements because she hadn't studied.

6. She didn't like that wheat bread because it tasted too sweet.

7. The doctor didn't give me an invoice because I didn't ask for it.

8. Martha didn't fire the clerk because he was married.

9. They didn't hurt the cubs because these were too young.

10. Xiomara didn't feel weak because she hadn't done any exercise.

Practice B. Complete the following conditions with the appropriate form of the verb in parenthesis. (Future and Past Conditions).

1. If the water is cool, I _**will take**_ a bath. (take)

2. If the program were updated, I _____ a copy. (buy)

3. I know i could earn more money if I _____ a better job. (find)

4. If the scale is increased, our profits _____. (rise)

5. We'll send you a bill if you _____ it. (request)

6. If the word processor doesn't work, our job _____ delayed. (be)

7. If the coast is clear, I _____ you a yell. (give)

8. They'll process your claim faster if you _____ it. (sign)

9. They would cover the entire market if they _____ a better product. (have)

10. If they _____ smart, they wouldn't use drugs. (be)

11. If they _____ the money, they'll keep it. (find)

12. If we _____ that movie, we might like it. (watch)

13. She could _____ us if she were closer. (see)

14. He would _____ to sleep if it weren't so early. (go)

15. We'll _____ you in the morning if we are interested. (call)

Reported Speech

Read the following conversations.

OSCAR: Where are you going in such a hurry?
EVELYN: I have to hurry or I'll miss my plane.
OSCAR: Are you traveling again?
EVELYN: Yes. I enrolled in a computer course for executives. It will be given in New York and my plane leaves at 5:00.
OSCAR: Well, I hope you enjoy your trip and the course. Good luck!

After Evelyn leaves, Oscar runs into Rick.

RICK: Were you just talking to Evelyn?
OSCAR: Yes, she just left.
RICK: What did she say?
OSCAR: She said she had to hurry or she would miss her plane.
RICK: Plane? Where is she going?
OSCAR: Well, she said she had enrolled in a computer course in New York.
RICK: Did she say what time her plane was leaving?
OSCAR: She told me it was leaving at 5:00.

 You have just read an example of **reported speech** in the second conversation. It simply means to convey (transmit) someone else's words to a third person.

Notice:

Evelyn said, "*I have to hurry or I'll miss my plane.*"
Oscar's words: "*She said she had to hurry or she would miss her plane.*"
Evelyn said, "*I enrolled in a computer course.*"
Oscar's words: "*She said she had enrolled in a computer course.*"

Oscar's words are examples of reported speech. He is telling Rick what Evelyn had said, but he's doing it using his own words.

Other examples:

David says, "This is my car."
Reported: David says that this is his car.
Erick says, "I have never seen her before."
Reported: Erick says that he has never seen her before.

Notice that the word THAT is optional.

The structure we just saw uses the verbs SAY and TELL in their present forms. Sometimes, however, we report speech using SAID or TOLD. Notice the difference:

Alex said, "My dad is here."
Alex said his dad was here.

She said, "I broke the lamp."
She said she had broken the lamp.

The woman told me, "I'm going to get well soon."
The woman told me she was going to get well soon.

He said, "I found the money."
He said he had found the money.

She said, "I have reached my goal."
She said she had reached her goal.

When we use SAID or TOLD, the verb from the statement we are reporting changes as follows:

FROM	CHANGES TO
present	past
will	would
can	could
may	might
was, were	had been
past	past perfect

WHAT WE HEAR:	**WHAT WE REPORT:**
He said, "I am...	He said he was...
They said, "We are...	They said they were...
She said, "I will...	She said she would...
He said, "I can...	He said he could...
They said, "We may...	They said they might...
He said, "I was robbed...	He said he had been robbed...
She said, "I took...	She said she had taken...
They said, "We broke...	They said they had broken...

Practice A. Write the reported speech based on the following sentences.

1. Cindy says, "I have seen Carmen's house."
2. The doctors say, "She will recover soon."
3. Irving says, "Evelyn's English has improved."
4. Some people say, "We are the best."
5. Peter says, "I like coconuts a lot."
6. My lawyer says, "His case is very complicated."
7. Steve says, "My lizard has died."

8. My brothers say, "We are happy to live alone."

9. Brenda says, "I can't understand French."

10. They say, "Our lives are much better now."

11. Walter says, "My mother is upset."

12. Victor says, "I love to swim."

13. Tony says, "My radio is broken."

14. Susan says, "I don't have a headache anymore."

15. Patty says, "I'm looking for a job."

Practice B. Write the reported speech based on the following sentences.

1. Karl said, "I feel tired."

2. The man said, "I have done my best."

3. Louis told me, "I saw the gleam in your eye."

4. My sisters said, "We settled the matter."

5. Miss Urrutia told him, "You swam very fast."

6. My mother said, "You steal my heart."

7. George told us, "We should merge the documents."

8. Your brother told me, "I sold the farm."

9. Edward said, "I love art."

10. His aunt said, "I am going away for a while."

11. Mark told her, "You shouldn't leave your house unlocked."

12. My niece told me, "You must be careful with ants."

13. Carol said, "I handled the payroll checks."

14. Your nephew said, "I have a thick book."

15. Mariela told me, "Your nails are very long."

Conversation Tidbits ✓

Do your best! Invent a story based on the photographs on this page. Share it with your classmates and teacher.

Business English and Conversation - Armando Aceituno M.

Chapter 6 — Other Structures Part II

Two-verb Structures

Look at these sentences:

1. I swim here
2. I want to swim here.
3. I love to swim here.
4. I love swimming here.
5. I insist on swimming here.

Sentence number **1** has only one verb. Its structure is the same as any other affirmative sentence.

Sentences **2** and **3** have two verbs working together, though there isn't anything strange in their structure.

Sentences **4** and **5**, however, use an "ing" form instead of the infinitive. This can only be done with certain verbs.

Now, let's see some rules.

a. When you have two verbs working together in a sentence, you need the particle "to" between them. This means you are using the infinitive of the second verb.

Examples:

> He wants to go home.
> She likes to control the petty cash.
> I need to buy a new car.

This can be done with verbs such as:

prefer	love	want
need	like	expect
hope	wish	try

b. With some verbs, you can use the "ing" form with the second verb instead of the infinitive.

Examples:

>He enjoys watching the news.
>I like skiing.
>She loves dancing, doesn't she?

Gerund

"ING" is the accepted form after the following verbs:

prefer	enjoy	begin	stop
love	like	go	quit
dislike	avoid	start	hate

c. Some verbs follow an entirely different pattern. For example, notice the usage of the following verbs:

>She **insisted on coming** by herself.
>We **desisted from trying** to convince him.
>I can't **remember going** to the store. (*I don't know whether I went to the store or not.*)

Practice A. Fill in the blanks with the verbs in parenthesis in their appropriate form.

1. Alex **_enjoys talking_** about saving the earth. (enjoy/talk)

2. Why does she _____ so much. (like/shop)

3. Manuel _____ prepaid shipments only. (prefer/send)

4. Does he _____ at 8:00? (start/work)

5. Miss Ross_____ the food. (hate/burn)

6. Did they_____ of their health? (quit/take care)

7. Annie doesn't_____the new ship. (want/see)

8. Why do you _____ insurance? (avoid/buy)

9. Jennie wouldn't _____, would she? (need/cheat)

10. They can't _____ how their revenues decrease. (like/watch)

Business English and Conversation - Armando Aceituno M.

Causatives

These are verbs which convey the idea of causing someone
to do something for someone else. There are very few verbs
which can be used in this manner, among them:

- ask   - order
- tell   - command
- instruct   - force
- make   - have

> She **made** him buy that medicine.
> He loves to **make** us suffer.
> **Make** him tell you the truth.

> She **had** him buy that medicine.
> We **had** him take the exam.
> The teacher **had** us give the report.

**ASK is the softest way of requesting something, of giving
an instruction.** It is considered very polite, lenient. We must
use the infinitive after ASK.

Examples:
> I asked Bob to check the copier.
> She asked me to call her during the weekend.
> They asked us to ignore the mistakes.
> We asked him not to bother us anymore.

Notice also that when we use pronouns, they must be in their
objective case (me, him, etc).

TELL is somewhat stronger than ASK. It gives the idea of
a higher authority issuing a soft order over its subordinates.

Examples:
> Mom told me to sit quietly.
> She told him to get lost.
> I told the secretary to check the reports twice.

Infinitives

INSTRUCT, ORDER, and COMMAND are similar, though Order and Command are a little bit stronger. They are both used in situations in which authority and/or superiority is undeniable or unavoidable.

Examples:

He ordered us to follow him.
The captain commanded his troops to stand at attention.
Did they order you to shut your mouth?

MAKE is used without the infinitive. It can be used when we cause someone to do something, though not necessarily by means of a much higher authority.

Examples:

Mom made me take a bath.
I made my sister eat the cake.
Daniel made me tell him the truth.
Did you make your students repeat the essay?
I naturally made him drink vinegar.
We didn't make him bite that garlic.

FORCE means exactly that: to make someone do something against his will.

Examples:

He forced her to unlock the safe.
Did she force you to leave?
The officers forced the crowd to disperse.

HAVE is not a very strong verb. It is similar in meaning to Make.

Examples:

Have the truck pick up the trash.
I had the students repeat the exam.
Could you have this package taken to our Main Street branch? (_Could you instruct someone to take the package?_)

Infinitive
_(to)_
_no_

Business English and Conversation - Armando Aceituno M.

Practice A. Complete each sentence with the appropriate form of ASK, TELL, MAKE, ORDER, or COMMAND, whichever completes the thought best. Some sentences may be completed with more than one of the options.

1. I _____ Mary to help me.
2. When I was outside, Mom _____ me to stop jumping.
3. General McDowell _____ his troops to advance.
4. She _____ me tell her everything.
5. The teacher _____ us to be quiet.
6. Did he _____ you follow him to the shop?
7. We _____ the delivery truck to take our furniture back.
8. I didn't _____ my brother to leave the room.
9. He didn't _____ you eat that stale bread, did he?
10. I _____ my boss to sign the documents.

Practice B. Fill in the blanks with one of the verbs from the list below. Use the past form only. Most sentences have more than one correct answer. Each verb should be used no more than twice.

Ask	Tell	Make	Command	Force	Instruct

1. Ronald _____ me to be careful.
2. I _____ her to leave.
3. Abraham _____ us not to return the bags.
4. They _____ him to crash against the wall.
5. Monica _____ me lose my balance.
6. The commander _____ us to remain silent.
7. Genevieve _____ the girls get out.
8. That officer _____ the guys to sit.
9. Frank _____ them sell their cars.
10. My boss _____ me to fire the secretary.
11. Edgar _____ us to check the bike.
12. Your mother _____ you to eat those vegetables.
13. Brenda _____ me to lend her some money.
14. The teacher _____ us to study.
15. Ernest _____ her practice English.

Capitalization

Using capital letters properly is important in correspondence. Always capitalize:

- " The first word in a sentence, quotation, salutations, attention lines, and closing lines
- " Proper nouns
- " Nouns before numbers which denote order, registration
- " Important words in an outline
- " Brand names or trademarks
- " Names of stars and planets
- " Names of holidays and other special events
- " Nationalities,
- " Governmental units
- " Specific academic degrees
- " Titles of books, movies, etc.

The first word of a sentence:

That truck is going very fast.

The first word of a quotation:

He said, "Where are they now?"
She said, "They think the flower is dead."

The first word and other important words in salutations, attention lines, and closing lines:

Dear Mr. Edson:
Attention: Planning Manager
Sincerely yours,

Proper Nouns:

Lone Fox Office	South Carolina
Monday	January
Tuesday	December

Nouns before numbers, if they show order, registration, etc:

Room 533   Flight 747   Chapter 2

Important words in an outline:

A. Introduction
    1. Welcome
    2. Special Announcements
B. Development
    1, Topic Presentation
    2. Discussion

Brand names and trademarks:

Jell-o   McDonald's

Names of stars and planets:

Venus   Uranus   Pluto

Exceptions: moon, sun, and earth.

Names of holidays and other special events:

Christmas	Independence Day
Interfer	Winter Festival

Nationalities and titles, when these precede the name:

Colombian	Guatemalan
Ambassador Black	Mayor Evans

Governmental units

Superior Court   State Senate

Specific academic degrees

B.S.   Bachelor of Science

Titles of books, movies, etc.

Batman XV   Titanic II

Practice A. Underline or circle all the words which should be capitalized in the following paragraphs.

1. computers are now an important part of our daily lives. everywhere you go, you see stores displaying programs such as foxstar, wordpower, taxbase, and others. each week there seems to be a new computer on the market. we now have computers which are made by idm, orange, compact, sti, and thousands more. our world has changed! our lives have improved. or, have they?

2. do you realize how much transportation has changed in the past few centuries? just a few hundred years ago, people everywhere, and that includes america, africa, europe and asia, had to walk for even hundreds of miles if they wanted to get around. at least, that's what history books tell us.

one such book is "the illustrated history of modern transportation," available on paperback from zarantroop publishing house. it is nicely bound and sells for only $25.00, which makes it one of the cheapest books of its kind available anywhere. if you enjoy reading historical facts, you'll like this book.

A. <u>Underline</u> **the embedded questions in the following sentences.**

   1. I'd like to know who misplaced the keys.
   2. She doesn't know where the files are.
   3. He can't explain why he took the money.
   4. Do you know who is coming to dinner?
   5. Tell me where Dony saw the car.

B. Complete the following conditions (future and present) using the appropriate form of the verb in parenthesis.

1. If he cleans the car, it _____ more. (shine)

2. Victor will insure his house if he _____ the price. (like)

3. If she attached documents properly, we _____ them. (receive)

4. If they _____ a cheaper jacket, they'll buy it. (find)

5. If I could change my speech, I _____ it. (do)

6. She _____ her profits if we were nice to her. (share)

7. If I reach a very old age, I _____ a grouchy man. (be)

8. If Hector jumped too high, he _____ off the stage. (fall)

9. They won't call the shareholders if you _____ them. (help)

10. If Luis _____ more on his credit card, he would have a bigger debt. (charge)

C. In your notebook or orally, make a condition (past unreal) based on each of the following statements. Most of these can be done correctly in more ways than one.

1. He didn't reach the top because he didn't try harder.
   <u>**If he had tried harder, he would've reached the top.**</u>
2. We dropped the statements because we weren't careful.
3. I didn't install the wall because I didn't have enough bricks.
4. She didn't go to college because she didn't speak English.
5. I didn't buy more stock because I didn't like the company.

119

D. Orally or in writing, change the following statements to reported speech.

1. Mike said, "I have vital information."
2. Gerald said, "I'll send you some copies."
3. Benjamin told me, "I want to be a stockholder."
4. They said, "We'll keep the subsidy going."
5. Yvette told us, "I have sent the telex."
6. She said, "The tenants aren't moving yet."
7. Lorena said, "I don't know who the trustee is."
8. My sister told me, "All street vendors are closed."
9. Carlos told them, "The verdict isn't fair."
10. The boss said, "The certificate is void."

E. Complete the sentences with the appropriate form and pattern of the verbs in parenthesis.

Infinitives or Gerunds

1. Karina never __**tried to improve**__ her handwriting. (try/improve)
2. They _____ the comic strips. (enjoy/read)
3. Marielos _____ me with this. (want/help)
4. We _____ to leave early. (dislike/have)
5. Laura _____ English someday. (need/learn)
6. I _____ to gossip. (avoid/listen)
7. Deborah _____ her clothes at last. (start/wash)
8. He _____ a diploma. (expect/receive)
9. Eugene finally _____ a pushover. (quit/be)
10. Does Michael _____? (hope/graduate)
11. Leslie doesn't _____ called "Less." (like/be)
12. What time do you _____? (stop/work)
13. Lucy _____ you. (wish/see)
14. Liz _____ at 7:00 (start/run)
15. George _____ on ice. (like/dance)

Business English and Conversation - Armando Aceituno M.

F. Orally or in writing, change the following sentences from active to passive voice.

1. William enclosed the brochure.
2. We supplied enough money.
3. Christine drafted the letter last week.
4. He held his handkerchief steadily.
5. Arthur guided the group to the top of the cliff.
6. They deducted those investments and some contributions.
7. Vivian traded her old car for a new car.
8. I gave a detailed account of the events.
9. Paul audited their accounts.
10. The newspaper fired the editor.
11. John sent the businessman another applicant.
12. The government gave reliable information.
13. Brian hired capable people.
14. Our doctor solved all our problems.
15. Alex found trouble with animal research.

G. Circle all the words that need capitalization.

o. miralda, founder of black angel enterprises, has just published a new book entitled   "better health right now," at a price of only $32.50. this book, published in english and spanish versions simultaneously, is aimed at the middle class market. it pursues the definite objective of reaching all major metropolitan areas in the states of california, chicago, and new york. we definitely recommend mr. miralda's book. buy it.

Conversation Tidbits ✓

1
2

Write sentences using
reported speech based
on these photographs.
Discuss them with your
classmates and teacher.

4

3

Business English and Conversation - Armando Aceituno M.

Read the following paragraph.

> *Janet was really upset her father wasn't coming for Christmas even though Janet had offered to pay for the tickets he said he couldn't afford to take a vacation his job was too important for him at the moment.*

Does the paragraph make much sense? It might if it were spoken. During speech we make normal pauses, changes in the tone of our voice, etc. When we are writing, however, we have to tell the reader when to pause or stop. We do this through the proper use of punctuation marks.

In this section we'll see the normally accepted use of the period, comma, and semicolon.

 The period is one of the most frequently used forms of punctuation. It should be used:

1. At the end of most types of sentences.

Imperative	: Bring me the Thompson file.
Affirmative	: The coffee smells good.
Negative	: They just don't understand.
Embedded Question	: She asked why the baby was crying.
Polite Request	: Will you please send me two samples.

Some writers prefer to use a question mark at the end of polite requests, but that is not very common.

2. After abbreviations:

Mr.   Dr.   Ph.D. Jr.   Sr.

3. As a decimal point:

$50.44   1.5 pounds   10.5 percent

, **The comma** is even more frequently used than the period. Because of this, there is disagreement pertaining some of its uses. We shall take a look at its more common ones.

---

1. Separating items in a list.

She found coffee, cotton, silk, and wool.
A secretary should type, file, answer the phone, etc.
He was good at singing, dancing, drawing, and computer programming.

2. To separate an appositive.

Miss Johnson, our representative, will call on you.
Roses, which are scarce around here, are expensive.
My neighbor, Mr. Davis, is a grouchy man.

3. To set off the name of a person being addressed.

Bob, I know you can do it.
I'd do anything for you, Vanessa.
With those drawings, James, we'll finish the project.

4. Before a tag question.

You sent the shipment, didn't you?
She was a good manager, wasn't she?
Dave has the report, doesn't he?

5. Before the abbreviations Jr., Sr., Inc., and Ltd.

David Smith, Sr., is our best salesperson.
Robert Boards, Inc., sent the order yesterday.
Walter Davids, Jr., came to see us last week.

6. **To separate a word or phrase which interrupts a sentence (causes a pause).**

> I think, therefore, that your statement is untrue.
> Personally, I think you're mistaken.
> However, many people like the game.
> Many people, however, liked the game.

7. **In and after a date. Notice.**

> The meeting of September 2, 2001, was the most boring.
> Your letter of Tuesday, August 4, has been received.

8. **To separate introductory clauses.**

> Now that John has returned, things will go back to normal.
> If she is busy, I'll come back later.
> As you know, our prices have increased.

Practice A. Insert commas and periods wherever necessary in the following memo. Then underline any words which should be capitalized.

yes fellow members of the mayan sales club year-end is fast approaching which means that our busiest season is just around the corner

we want to improve our sales performance from last year that's why we are going to offer great discounts in all our departments special emphasis will be made on sporting goods home appliances ladies' wear and office equipment

there will be a 15% discount on sales made during mondays and wednesdays this discount however does not apply to season greeting cards which are already being offered at substantial savings

; | The semicolon should be used:

1. Between simple sentences which are not joined by a coordinating conjunction (for, but, and, nor, or, yet).

All the schools were ready; the parade began.
I gave my report to the committee; they read it without making any comments.
Some students try to cheat on every exam; others try to prepare themselves by studying.

2. Before adverbs such as nevertheless, however, therefore, and moreover, when they are joining two independent clauses.

This is a company problem; nevertheless, it should be discussed with the employees.
I don't like to be harsh with you; however, you leave me no choice.

3. Before expressions such as FOR EXAMPLE, NAMELY, and THAT IS.

They have many options; for example, New York, Chicago, or Honolulu.
I pointed out his worst defect; namely, that he never admits he's wrong.
He went astray; that is, he chose not to listen to us.

Practice B. Insert semicolons where needed.

1. He opened the door however, he found no one inside.

2. His thoughts were pure nevertheless, nobody trusted him.

3. They were always saying bad things about him namely, that he was not sincere.

4. He cared about many people for example, his girlfriend.

5. She believed him however, she couldn't do much for him.

6. He packed all his belongings he packed all his dreams.

7. He headed for the station he didn't say a word to anyone.

8. She felt like crying nevertheless, she didn't try to stop him.

9. She saw him get on the train he never turned to look back.

10. She saw the train disappear in the distance she felt her life ending.

Practice C. Insert all needed punctuation marks in the following reading.

so whenever tameless wanted to see herself in a mirror, she had to go to matchless' house. but hopeless wasn't the only problem that tameless had to face. dipless and reckless, her mean ugly half-sisters also made life impossible for her, especially dipless who liked to play cruel jokes on tameless.

one day, or actually one night, while everybody was sleeping, dipless slipped into tameless' bedroom and dyed her hair purple. this wouldn't have mattered, except that purple was the color that tameless hated most, since her half-sisters' eyes were also purple. when tameless woke up, she saw her long purple hair. she then ran to speechless' house, and her friend, upon seeing tameless' hair, became even more speechless.

tameless was angry. she had to get even, but she didn't know what to do. so she called some of her other friends and they all met at matchless' house and conceived the perfect plan to get revenge on dipless. they saw, however, that this was a chance to get even also with hopeless and reckless.

■
■ It is rather simple to use the colon

1. **To introduce a list of items or an idea.** Usually, when we have the words AS FOLLOWS, THE FOLLOWING, SUCH AS THESE, introducing a series of items, we need a colon.

We need the following supplies:
Pencils, erasers, books, and note pads.

The following people have been laid off:
Herbert Stevens
Richard Davis
Judy Kestler

2. **After the salutation in a business letter, except when you are using open punctuation.**

Dear Mr. Melgar: Dear Mrs. Mueller:
Gentlemen: Dear Sir:

■ ■ ■ The ellipses are a series of dots used to indicate that part of the text has been omitted.

1. **When a segment is omitted within a passage.**

Then the truth matters not, ... it sets us free.
...as Laura... walked a little faster.

2. **When a statement is left unfinished.**

I think Dony is right, but Ralph...

3. **If the omission is at the end of a sentence, use the ellipses and the proper end punctuation.**

> Can you tell me why...?
> She never answered because....

— | **The hyphen is used:**

1. **To divide a word which doesn't fit completely at the end of the line.**

   All the programs look interesting but extremely difficult to master.

2. **To form some compound nouns.**

   mother-in-law   self-control   step-father

▬▬▬ | **The dash is used in several ways.**

1. **To indicate a break in the thought being expressed.**
   The ghost —and I know it was a ghost— came into the
   room.

2. **To separate nonessential material.**
   Bob Parker —you knew him as "Bugsy"— died today.

3. **To emphasize a descriptive or explanatory phrase.**
   We are introducing our new product —Stanley Raisin
   Grapes.

? **The question mark is needed:**

1. After a direct question.

Did our prospective buyer show up?
When does our plane arrive?
Why are you here?

2. After a tag question.

She has sufficient data, doesn't she?
He gathered the information, didn't he?
They'll import the leather goods, won't they?

 The exclamation point is used after a word, phrase or sentence which expresses a strong emotion.

"We aren't going!" they said.
Such a great morning!

Do not overuse the exclamation point in this way:

That's great!!!

 The quotation marks have several uses. Among them:

1. To enclose a direct quotation.

Bill said, "Business is not the same."
"You're crazy," said Claudia.

2. To enclose the title of an article or chapter.

I read the article on "The Ozone Layer" in this month's Journal of Science.

3. Around unusual words or phrases.

She says that "ain't" is not correct and should not be used.

4. To enclose definitions.

I think "love at first sight" is nonexistent.

With other punctuation:

1. A final period or comma is placed inside the quotation marks.

"I think," he said, "you are right."

2. Final semicolons and colons are placed outside the quotation marks.

She enjoyed the article "A Crusade"; however, she disagreed with the author on some points.

3. Question marks and exclamation points are placed inside the quotation marks when they are part of the quoted text.

He shouted, "Get out, you ruffians!"
She asked me, "Why are you sad this time?"
Did you ask her why she was watching "Love Story"?

I The apostrophe is used:

1. To show a contraction.

They'll bill me later.   (they will)
He'd done a good job.   (he had)
He'd like to try to survive. (he would)

2. To show possession.

The lady's bag.   (The bag of the lady.)
My Mom's car.   (The car of my Mom.)

3. To show some plurals, especially those pertaining to numerals, abbreviations, and letters.

People worked more in the 80's.
The A's were filed before the B's.

Practice D In the following sentences, insert the proper punctuation marks.

1. Dave Kingman a man after my own heart is a great businessman
2. My brother in law bought the adjacent house
3. We mustn't forget our primary purpose to sell
4. No vacancies we already knew that said the manager
5. We found the torn sheets but then

Practice E. Supply the missing punctuation marks. Rewrite the sentences in your notebook.

1. Albert asked Why is the soap on the floor
2. She tried to lower her eyes, but
3. Get out she shouted
4. It is a pleasure to announce our new cleaner Dust Proof
5. Whenever you try harder things get more complex

Chapter 8

Effective Communication

When you write a letter, a memo or any other type of written piece of information, you are communicating. Your communication should be effective; in other words, it should achieve its purpose.

What is the purpose of a written piece of business communication?

If may be one or more of the following:

To ask for information.   To advertise a product or service.
To provide information.   To convince
To order a product.   To request payment
etc.

Example 1. Asking for information.

Dear Sirs:

I would like to obtain information on your new exercise bench, Super Duper Gym. Please send me the list of items that you include with the equipment. I also need the prices on the different benches available.

The information may be sent to the address shown above. At the same time, you might send me any details on the credit and lay away options.

Sincerely yours,

Example 2. **Providing Information**

Thank you for your letter of August 7, in which you request information on our new exercise bench, Super Duper Gym. The enclosed catalog contains details on all the different benches available, as well as a complete price list.

Should you require more information, do not hesitate to call us. Our representative in your city will visit you shortly thereafter.

Cordially,

Example 3. Ordering a product.

Please send me two bottles of your Brainless Angel Vitamin. I would rather receive the smaller orange pills. A check for the total amount is enclosed.

It should be noted that order letters are not used much anymore. They have been slowly replaced by other ordering systems such as e-mail, fax, special forms, etc.

How can you make sure that your written communication is effective?

That's where proper style comes in. Read the following sentences.

1. I want you guys to send some of those catalogs you have.
2. Would you please send me a few catalogs so that we may browse through them.
3. Please send 3 catalogs to the address on the letterhead.

Sentence 1 = This type of language is acceptable in conversation but never in a formal letter.

Sentence 2 = Nicer language, but it provides unnecessary information.

Sentence 3 = Much better. To the point and specific.

There are several guidelines which will help you when writing.

1. BE SPECIFIC. Avoid using unnecessary words or providing nonessential information. Which of the following examples uses too many words to deliver the message?

a. My very dear cousin, June, who was born in Oklahoma City and has lived there for most of her fifty years, is coming over for a short visit sometime next month.

b. My cousin, June, from Oklahoma, is visiting me soon.

2. **BE CONCISE.** Get to the point as quickly and as clearly as possible. Make sure that your reader understands exactly what you want to tell him.

a. The boxes you sent, not the ones with the green labels but the ones with the orange labels, they were open (some of them) and the shoes were stained because all the ink containers from the shipment of another company spilled and stained the shoes in the boxes you sent.

b. Some of the boxes with green labels were open and the shoes therein contained were stained with ink from another shipment.

Both sentences say exactly the same thing, but the second one gets to the point quickly and clearly.

3. **USE VARIETY IN YOUR SENTENCES.** Your sentences should consist of no less than 5 or 6 words and no more than 20. Of course, there are exceptions; however, it is a good rule to follow since long sentences can be boring. Don't use only short or only long sentences; mix them.

Example:

> The van handled well, better than in her previous expeditions. Syvia felt that the advantage tonight was hers. The engine buzzed softly as the vehicle advanced quickly swallowing huge chunks of road with every passing second. The night vision system worked perfectly and she could see the slightest details on the highway in front of her.
>
> All three radars were active and doing their job with no glitches at all. The sensors indicated that no human or machine heat was detected for miles around. No human dwellings anywhere nearby. No vehicles of any type to be reckoned with for now.

4. **EXPAND YOUR VOCABULARY.** Most of us use the same words over and over. Try to have a dictionary and a thesaurus close at hand. Learn to use them well, since both can be of exceptional help in your writing.

Phrases, Fragments, Sentences

You must be able to distinguish between a sentence and a phrase, and between a phrase and a fragment.

PHRASE   :   The cat
FRAGMENT :   When the cat jumped
SENTENCE :   When the cat jumped, I got scared.

A phrase contains a subject without a verb. It may be very short or very long, but as long as it does not contain a verb, it remains a phrase.

> The position
> The position of General Manager
> The very desirable position of General Manager
>
> The wall
> The concrete wall
> The concrete wall on the other side of our fence

A fragment may contain a subject and a verb, but not a complete thought. It needs extra information to convey its real meaning. **Observe:**

> Although we have enough money to burn.
> Because it doesn't concern you.
> Since our operations were combined.
> When you paid her a compliment.
> Where the glasses fell.

A fragment usually begins with a conjunction (and, or, since, because, although, etc.) or an adverb (when, where, etc.).

137

A complete sentence, on the other hand, has a subject, a verb, and a complete thought. Notice the change when we incorporate the fragments to another clause.

> **Although we have enough money to burn**, we shouldn't waste it.
> I won't give you the report **because it doesn't concern you.**
> **Since our operations were combined**, our revenues have increased 15 percent.
> She smiled **when you paid her a compliment.**
> The floor is now messy **where the glasses fell.**
> **Looking for the right job**, Hector came into my office.

Practice A. Write P (Phrase), F (Fragment), or S (Sentence) in the space provided, whichever is appropriate.

P / F / S

1. _____ Peter was only 5 feet tall.
2. _____ But aggressive and hit hard.
3. _____ And he wanted to play.
4. _____ Carol expected to graduate with top honors.
5. _____ When the coaches expressed very little interest.
6. _____ The best defensive player on the team.
7. _____ Christian and all his hard-drinking pals.
8. _____ He won the trophy last year.
9. _____ He decided to quit the team.
10. _____ Elisa left already.
11. _____ Decided to give up football.
12. _____ After I finished the book, I went to sleep.
13. _____ Robert's grandmother and her club members.
14. _____ A habit which can lead to many problems.
15. _____ Those students have been very kind to me.

Practice B. In the space provided, write P (phrase), S (sentence), or F (fragment) as appropriate.

1. _____ In that very same kingdom.

2. _____ In the middle of the woods.

3. _____ A poor orphan named Tame Jane.

4. _____ She certainly was tame.

5. _____ Her hair was short and turned down.

6. _____ Her long and turned-up nose.

7. _____ And even if they had been the other way around.

8. _____ She wasn't a great beauty.

9. _____ She loved animals, and she was always kind to strange old ladies.

11._____ And she rode out of the palace in a hurry.

12._____ Right into the middle of the woods.

13._____ and was soon lost.

14. _____ She got off her horse and slapped it sharply for losing the way.

15. _____ The old, sad-looking horse which had always been so faithful.

16. _____ The horse said nothing, but ran right back home.

17. _____ It had known the way back all the time.

18. _____ Cinderella and her sad-looking horse.

19. _____ So there was the princess, lost in a dark wood.

20. _____ And she tried to tell the horse.

21. _____ Because the horse was very stubborn.

22. _____ She cried.

23. _____ At three o'clock, seven kids arrived.

24. _____ We drank all the milk, ate all the snacks, and used up all the napkins.

25. _____ But Mom only said , "Glad to have you all here."

Run-on sentences

Examine carefully the next two sentences.

> 1. The secretary misplaced some documents now she can't find them.
> 2. The secretary misplaced some documents; now, she can't find them.

Sentence 1 is a run-on sentence. It has two sentences which are incorrectly joined.

Sentence 2 presents the same statements separated by semicolon. Run-on sentences are a very common problem. Read the following examples of run-on sentences:

> 1. I saw Gladiator IV last week at home today I'm going to see Gladiator V.
>
> 2. Some of the children are nice Beatrice likes playing with them in the backyard.
>
> 3. Their parents never came to see them this hurt the little children a lot.

Sentence 1 should have a punctuation mark between HOME and TODAY. Look at the following correct options.

> **a.** I saw Gladiator IV last week at home, and today I'm going to see Gladiator V.
> **b.** I saw Gladiator IV last week at home; I'm going to see Gladiator V today.
> **c.** I saw Gladiator IV last week at home. Today I'm going to see Gladiator V.

Sentence 2 should contain punctuation between NICE and BEATRICE.

a. Some of the children are nice; that's why Beatrice enjoys playing with them.
b. Some of the children are nice, and Beatrice enjoys playing with them.
c. Some of the children are nice. Beatrice enjoys playing with them.

The break in sentence 3 occurs between THEM and THIS.

a. Their parents never came to see them; this hurt the little children a lot.
b. Their parents never came to see them, and this hurt the little children a lot.
c. Their parents never came to see them. This hurt the little children a lot.

Comma Splice	*I like Beethoven, however, I think Chopin was better.*

The previous sentence has insufficient punctuation. It has what is called a **comma splice** between "Beethoven" and "however". The punctuation mark needed in this case is a semicolon.

I like Beethoven; however, I think Chopin was Better.

We can also correct the comma splice with a conjunction.

I like Beethoven, **but** I think Chopin was better.

Notice the following examples of sentences with insufficient punctuation.

1. Many stories are based on fact there are people who still doubt their veracity.
2. Jane thought she wanted to study medicine, she went to law school instead.
3. Rick wanted to give her a diamond ring, he couldn't afford it.

These can be corrected as follows:

Many stories are based on fact, **but** there are people who still doubt their veracity.

1   **Although** many stories are based on fact, there are people who doubt their veracity.

Many stories are based on fact; **however,** there are people who doubt their veracity.

Jane thought she wanted to study medicine, **but** she went to law school instead.

2   **Even though** Jane wanted to study medicine, she went to law school.

Jane wanted to study medicine; **however,** she went to law school instead.

Rick wanted to give her a diamond ring, **but** he couldn't afford it.

3   Rick wanted to give her a diamond ring; **alas,** he couldn't afford it.

Although Rick wanted to give her a diamond ring, he couldn't afford it.

Remember, you can correct comma splices in several ways:

- With a comma and a conjunction (but, for, and, etc.)
- With a semicolon
- With a period
- By using a conjunction at the beginning of the sentences (although, even, though, etc)

Practice A. Underline or circle the place where the break occurs in each sentence.

1. She has been a manager for five long years she earned her title through hard work.
2. You should never doubt his word he may be telling you the truth now.
3. Many people stop on this road they always disappear.
4. Apparently a girl fell off the bridge into the river her body was never found.
5. Some students try to cheat the teacher always catches them.
6. A mysterious light appears in the mountain at midnight I have seen it.
7. The boss called her to his office after lunch she was a bag of nerves.
8. I misjudged her she seemed so fragile the first time I met her.
9. He loves playing chess in the afternoon he does it every day.
10. They managed to avoid conflict it seemed inevitable at first.

Practice B. Correct the following sentences to eliminate the comma splice in each.

1. Lucy bought a brand new car yesterday, it was very expensive and fast.
2. There was a real race the next day, naturally, this was what she wanted.
3. She drove the car to school, she parked it near the campus.

4. Proud of her car, Lucy drove it to the park, she felt really great.

5. When she left her car unlocked, she left the keys inside, it was stolen.

6. Someone had stolen it, the thief now owned a rather fast car.

7. Lucy was extremely angry, she hit with a bat the first car she saw.

8. This was an unusual thing for her to do, Lucy isn't a troublemaker.

9. She tried to find the owner, she was unable to do so.

10. She took the bat and threw it in the trash, the garbage truck picked it up the next day.

Practice C. Insert all needed punctuation marks.

1. In a country not so far away there lived a king this king had three sons.
2. John was the oldest Ben was next and Billy was the youngest.
3. A little girl also lived in the place her name was Wendy.
4. She was the child of the king's friend who had died she was really beautiful.
5. The king cared for her as if she were his own he took her everywhere he went.
6. As the four children grew up they came to love one another.
7. When they were old enough all three wanted Wendy to be his wife.
8. The princess herself could not choose among the three she loved all of them.
9. The king wanted one of the boys to marry Wendy he really liked her.
10. After much thought the king called his sons to him he had made a decision.

Paragraphs

Writing a paragraph is simple; you just put a few sentences together, right?

Well, yes, and no.
Yes, a paragraph is a group of related sentences.
No, it's not that simple. Read the following paragraphs.

1. I went to your store on Wednesday, January 4. I purchased a leather jacket for $150.00 and a wooden chair for $15.00. In addition, I bought seven bottles of white wine, ten boxes of nails and three hammers. Now I see your invoice and it says that I purchased a lot more than I really did, and that's a mistake because I have all the receipts to prove otherwise.

2. I received your bill for purchases. The total amount shown of $1,244.00 is incorrect. My records indicate an amount of $396.34. We seem to have a discrepancy.

3. I received your invoice for purchases made on January 29. It shows several transactions for a total of $1,244.00, while my records indicate that the total should be $496.00.

The previous three paragraphs would be found in a letter of claim. What do you notice about them?

" Paragraph 1 is too blunt and rude.
" Paragraph 2 is not as rude, but it is "choppy" because it contains only short sentences.
" Paragraph 3 seems more polite and clearer, and it uses short and long sentences.

To write effective paragraphs, you need to remember a few things.

1. **Be clear and concise.** It is particularly advisable to include a **topic sentence;** this should be the first sentence in the paragraph.
   Example:

> Sales of leather goods have decidedly declined in recent years. Some manufacturers have reported that their sales for the fiscal year ending March 1, have declined by as much as 35%. No one seems to understand the reasons for such a huge drop in the demand for leather articles.

What is the topic of this paragraph?

You probably answered correctly: The decline in sales of leather goods. A topic sentence needs to be included in the paragraph to give the reader an idea of what we are talking about.

2. **Vary your sentences.** Use short and long sentences, simple and compound ones. Try different patterns.

Examples.

> 1. I have discussed the plan with my assistant, and we feel that there are several improvements which could be made.

> 2. After discussing the plan, my assistant and I feel that several improvements are necessary.

> 3. My assistant and I feel that several improvements are needed on the plan.

4. The plan has been discussed extensively. My assistant and I feel that some improvements should be made.

Practice A. Change the order of the following sentences (if necessary) and combine them to make complete paragraphs. Write each completed paragraph in your notebook. Make any changes concerning structure, wording, etc., that you consider necessary.

GROUP A

1. Meanwhile, the guests are beginning to demand a lot more from the hostess.

2. Although wine and whiskey have already been served in addition to the beer.

3. The best beer has been bought for this party.

4. Many people were invited to this wedding.

5. Even with their demands, we will have a wonderful time.

GROUP B

1. Others, however, wait at least 18 months to even try walking.

2. Some grow much faster than others.

3. Some can walk by the time they are 11 months old.

4. It has been shown that no two babies are alike.

5. There are also some who can talk fluently at an early age.

GROUP C

1. Then you put the eggs in a frying pan.

2. Then you fry the eggs to your liking.

3. This frying pan should contain oil.

4. Making fried eggs is really simple.

5. First, you take two eggs and crack their shells.

Optional Practice. Write paragraphs based on one or more of the photographs on this page.

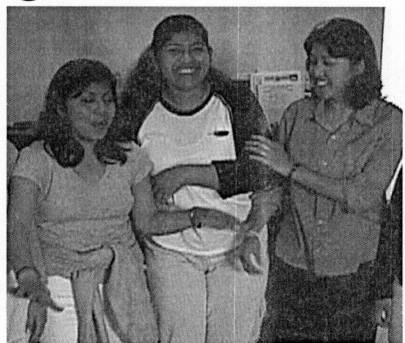

Business English and Conversation - Armando Aceituno M.

PART II

Correspondence

A normal dictionary may define correspondence this way:

Correspondence *n*. 1. Communication by letters or other documents

Perhaps the most important word in that definition is COMMUNICATION. It is important to emphasize this, because clear, concise and efficient communication is essential in today's business world. And it is not limited to letters, because it includes telephone calls, faxes, and perhaps most important of all: electronic mail (e-mail).

For most types of correspondence, however, it is best to follow these guidelines.

Ö Be specific. Don't fill the letter with a lot of unimportant details.
Ö Be complete. At the same time, tough, do not be so brief that you forget the important information.
Ö Be courteous. Make sure that the language you use is polite.
Ö Electronic mail (e-mail) should be especially short and to the point.

This section of the book contains the following areas:

" Parts of the Letter
" Styles of Letters
" Types and Samples of Letters

Chapter 9 | Parts of the Letter

A normal letter is typed on standard-size paper, which will vary depending on the region you live in. For instance, in most areas of America, the standard size is also known as letter-size which measures 8 1/2 by 11 inches. In Europe and other areas, the standard size varies. For instance, you may use A4, which is somewhat larger than letter-size, or any other formats which may exist in your area.

As far as e-mail is concerned, most electronic mail servers use a standard form which usually contains the same parts, although in different format.

FOR PRINTED LETTERS

The style and margins will usually depend on:

" The preferences and rules of your organization
" The type and size of the document
" Other considerations

The following pages contain diagrams of the main parts of a business letter. The common parts are the following:

USUAL PARTS
Letterhead
Date Line
Inside Address
Salutation Line
Body
Complimentary Closing
Signature
Initials

OPTIONAL PARTS
Typed Heading
Attention Line
Subject Line
Enclosures
Carbon Copies
Postscript

Usual Parts

(Placement will vary with style.
Optional Parts in italics)

Letterhead

Typed
Heading

Date Line

Inside
Address

Salutation Line

or Attention Line

Subject Line

Body

Complimentary Closing

Signature

Initials

Enclosures
Carbon Copies
Postscript

The Letterhead

Most professional letterheads include:

- The company's name and address
- A telephone, telex, or fax number
- E-mail address and/or website
- Other information

The style of the letterhead varies from company to company. It really depends on the preferences of the organization and those in charge of designing it. That is why there is no standard measurements or format.

Examples:

Westinghouse Industries, Inc.
* Electronics
* Appliances
* Auto Parts

373 Willard Blvd. Los Angeles, CA 90044
westinghouse.com

 Servitec International
555 Western St.
Miami, FL 98322

The Date Line

It is commonly typed on the fifteenth line from the top of the page, but this depends on the size of the letter being prepared.

The date should be written out completely, not just with numbers. This is done to avoid confusion, since in some areas, 08-01-01 means August 1, 2001, while in others it means January 8, 2001.

CORRECT	INCORRECT
April 15, 2001	4-15-01 or 15-4-01
July 9, 2001	7-9-01 or 9-7-01
April 20, 2001	20 of April, 2001

Typed Heading

If the paper doesn't have a letterhead, you may need to type a heading with your return address and the date line, beginning on line 13 or 14 (depending on the length of the letter). The sender's name may be included, but this is optional.

Jessica Olive
233 Southern Ave
Los Angeles, CA 90063
April 15, 2001

Inside Address

This part of the letter contains addressee's name and title, street address, city, state and zip code. It is typed five or six lines below the date line, at the left margin.

Mr. Robert Williams
Sales Manager
Queen Corporation
Chicago, IL 09382

Mrs. Celia Zent, President
COOP, Inc.
189 Northern Drive
Philadelphia, PA 20014

If a title and a degree specify the same thing, do not combine.

INCORRECT
Dr. Jessica Olive, M.D.

Dr. Alex Bochart, Ph. D.

CORRECT
Dr. Jessica Olive
Jessica Olive, M.D.

Dr. Alex Bochart
Alex Bochart, Ph. D.

Outside Address

This is the address that is typed on the envelope, and it should be exactly the same as the inside address. It is typed approximately a half inch from the top, near the center of the envelope.

Salutation

It is typed two lines after the inside address or the attention line.

Dear Mr. Thomas: Dear Sir:
Dear Madam: Dear Dr. Conroy:
Gentlemen: Dear Mrs. Jones:

Optional Practice. Write the appropriate inside addresses based on each group of data. Include all the necessary parts and use the common format.

1. Mr. John Smith, Manager, West Technology, Inc., P.O. Box 280, Boulder, CO, 80321-0001
2. Alex Botz, Ph. D., Dartmouth College, 124 Dixie Blvd., Orlando, Florida, 32069

The Body

This is the most important part of the business letter, because it contains the message. It should begin two lines after the salutation or subject line. When the letter is very short, you can use double spacing with all parts of the letter.

The paragraphs can be aligned with the left margin, indented, or "hanging", depending on the style you are using. A medium-sized letter will contain two or three paragraphs separated each by a blank line.

Continuation Line

This is sometimes used when the letter is too long and doesn't fit in one page, so we have to continue the text on a second sheet of paper, which may or may not contain a letterhead. It is typed about an inch from the top of the page, and it should contain the addressee's name, the page number, and the date:

Jessica Olive   **August 3, 2001**   **Page 2**

Closing

It is typed on the second line below the body.

Examples:

Truly yours,	Very truly yours,
Sincerely yours,	Cordially
Cordially yours	Sincerely,

Signature

It is typed four or five lines after the closing. It may include the writer's name and title, as well as the name of a department or division of the company.

Herman Downey
Sales Manager

Initials

They are typed two lines after the signature, but aligned with the body (without indention). The author's initials are typed in capitals and the typist's initials are typed in small letters. They can be separated by a colon or a slash.

OM:ml   IY/wy   BC:pr

Enclosures

If we have to send other documents with the letter, we must tell the reader by including an enclosures notation, which is typed two lines after the initials.

Enclosures:
1 invoice
1 catalog

Carbon Copies

When you send a copy or photocopy of the letter to another person, you must use this notation. It is common in some areas to type "cc" for carbon copy or "c" for electronic copy or regular photocopy, two lines below the initials or other notation.

c: Julius Johnson

Postscript

Business letters should never include a postscript. But if it ever becomes necessary, then type the notation **P.S.** or **p.s.** two lines below the last reference you have in your letter, then include the additional information.

P.S. The gray cubicles look much better now.

Letter Styles

The more common letter styles in existence today are:

Full-block	Blocked	Semi-blocked
Indented	Simplified	Hanging-indented

The Semi-blocked and Blocked styles are more popular, although many organizations are using the Simplified style.

    " The simplified style saves typing time. It doesn't have salutation nor closing, and the parts are all at the left margin. It does have a subject line, and the writer's name is written out in capitals.

    " The indented and hanging-indented styles are not in use anymore.

Punctuation Styles

As far as punctuation is concerned, there exist three styles:

Open, Standard and Closed

but only two are widely used today.

    " The open punctuation has only the commas, periods, and other marks used within the body, but nothing in the other parts of the letter.

" The standard punctuation uses a colon after the salutation and a comma after the closing.

" Closed punctuation has a period after the date line, commas after each line of the inside address and typed heading (if any), and period after the last line of the same. It also has a colon after the salutation, comma after the closing, and a period after the last line of the signature and initials. It is not used much anymore.

Full-block

April 20, 2001

Miss Mariza Baldwin
Blessed Industries
777 N. Heavens Drive
Los Angeles, CA 90777

Dear Miss Baldwin:

This is a letter typed using the full-block (which some authors call "full-blocked") style with standard punctuation. It is widely used today, although many writers prefer to indent the paragraphs which would then convert it into a cross between a full-block and semi-blocked-styled letter.

The actual style most secretaries and other business writers will use depends largely on the preferences of the company they are working for. Most companies prefer to use blocked or semi-blocked style, but there are some who like to use the simplified style as well.

Sincerely yours,

Armando Aceituno M.

Blocked

April 20, 2001

Miss Mariza Baldwin
Blessed Industries
777 N. Heavens Drive
Los Angeles, CA 90777

Dear Miss Baldwin

This is a letter typed using the blocked style with open punctuation. It is not used much today, since many writers prefer to indent the paragraphs which would then convert it into a semi-blocked-styled letter.

It is important to remember that the actual style most secretaries and other business writers use depends, among other factors, on the preferences of the company they are working for. Most companies prefer to use blocked or semi-blocked style.

Sincerely yours

Armando Aceituno M.

Semi-blocked

April 20, 2001

Miss Mariza Baldwin,
Blessed Industries,
777 N. Heavens Drive,
Los Angeles, CA 90777.

Dear Miss Baldwin:

    This is a letter typed using the semi-blocked style with closed punctuation. It is used a lot today, since many writers prefer to indent the paragraphs which converts it from a blocked-styled letter.

    It is important to remember that the actual style most secretaries and other business writers use depends, among other factors, on the preferences of the company they are working for. Most companies prefer to use blocked or semi-blocked style.

        Sincerely yours,

        Armando Aceituno M.

Chapter 10 — Types of Letters

Letter of Inquiry

This is the letter that you would send if you need information on something. You can also use it to clear any doubts you may have or to ask for special favors.

These are some ways in which you can begin and end a letter of this type.

> I need information on...
> We need the following information:
> Would you please...
> Please send me...
> I will be grateful if you...
> We will be grateful for your help...
> Thank you for your cooperation...
> I will appreciate this help...

Optional Practice. Write the body of a letter of inquiry to fit the following situation.

You saw an ad for an item you liked and you are interested in buying one. You write to the manufacturer because you want the name of the nearest dealer, as well as models and prices. Include all the normal parts of the letter, except letterhead.

Sample Letter of Inquiry 1:

> We are seeking advertising and promotional ventures for our organization. After reading the last few issues of your publication, it appears that we may have a common audience.
>
> To help us make our decision, please send your publication's media kit. It can be forwarded to our main office. Please be sure to include your advertising rates and circulation data, including a complete breakdown of complimentary and paid subscriptions.
>
> We look forward to receiving your literature.

Sample Letter of Inquiry 2:

> Dear Mrs. Flowers:
>
> Karen Zelada, who works in your sales department, has mentioned that your organization is looking for a competent sales manager. I believe I have the qualifications to fill that opening satisfactorily.
>
> I have had two years of training at Nitrogen Sales School and have achieved a high grade point average. While in school, I worked part time in the main office as a sales supervisor. I enjoyed my work and am confident that I can adequately fill your vacancy.
>
> My résumé is enclosed, but if you need any additional information, you may reach me at 132-5566 any day after 6:00 p.m. I hope to have the privilege of a personal interview at your earliest convenience.

Optional Practice - Answer the letter from Sample Letter 2

Practice A. Write the body of a letter of inquiry to fit the following situation: You want information on office furniture. Request a catalog with models, prices and other pertinent information.

Letter of Reply

After we receive a letter of inquiry, we send a letter of reply. When you send this type of letter, be sure to provide all the information requested and send it as promptly as possible.

This type of letter may be used for one or more of the following purposes.

- Ö Answer specific questions
- Ö Provide required information
- Ö Provide a positive or negative response
- Ö Clear doubts

Sample Letter of Reply

Dear Mrs. Linares:

Thank you for giving me an opportunity to read the manuscript of your new novel, "Free, For Ever Free." Several people on the editorial staff have read the manuscript, and they all found it extremely good.

Unfortunately, our company can only publish two or three novels each year. Since it would be unfair of us to keep your manuscript, we are returning it with the hope that you can sell it elsewhere.

Sincerely yours,

Practice B. Write the original letter of inquiry which Sample Letter 2 seems to answer. In other words, you are sending a manuscript of a novel for an editor to review and consider for publication.

Order Letter

This letter is used to purchase products or services. Most companies, however, now have standard forms which are used instead of this type of letter. Others simply use internet to handle all their purchases.

It is essential that the information you provide be accurate, so you don't receive the wrong items.

Sample Order Letter

> To confirm our conversation of last week, please send us three small APCO 158 sound systems and amplifiers. They should be delivered at our Chicago office. The address is on the letterhead.
>
> The invoice should be sent to our Accounting Department at 345 S. Hampton Ave., Los Angeles, CA 90332.
>
> If you have any questions about this order please refer them to Michael Lorraine, Purchasing Manager, at 188-3233.

Letter of Acknowledgement

This type of letter is used to acknowledge the one or more of the following:

- Ö Documents received
- Ö Order or payments received
- Ö Favors granted
- Ö Appointments made
- Ö Agreements reached

It shows courtesy to write this type of letter. It tells the addressee that you have received whatever it was that he sent you. It also avoids confusion and misunderstanding. The customer wants to know when he's going to receive his order. The acknowledgment letter tells him whether you have the products available and when you are going to send them.

Last but not least, this letter provides a record for your business. The copy you keep of this letter reminds you of when you are supposed to send the merchandise.

Sample Letter of Acknowledgement:

Dear Mrs. Delly:

Thank you for writing us about the video cassette recorders that you wish to return. After receiving your letter with the items, we checked them and found that some of the wiring had been damaged during the transportation.

To make sure that you have no more problems, we are sending you three completely new video cassette recorders. You should receive them sometime in the next few weeks. Please accept them with our apologies for any inconvenience you may have suffered.

If you need further assistance, please do not hesitate to contact us.

Collection Letter

Sometimes people need to be reminded that their account or payment on a loan is past due.

It is rather difficult to write this type of letter letter, because it must be very tactful and courteous. It is usually sent in a series:

1. Gentle reminder that the account is overdue.
2. Stronger reminder.
3. Urgent request to make a payment.
4. Threat of legal action (ultimatum).
5. Letter from attorney or collection agency.

Sample Letter 1 (gentle reminder):

Dear Mr. Letterman:

We understand that life can be really hectic at times, and we neglect even our most important habits. For instance, we can neglect the important tradition of sending our payments on time.

Your organization does have an obligation to Duvall Publishers, too. Your credit history suggests that your lack of promptness in remitting payment to us must be due to simple neglect. Our records indicate that the amount of $893.25 is currently past due by sixty days.

If this letter crossed paths with your check, please accept our apologies for this friendly reminder. We simply would like to revitalize your company's good habits before the situation gets out of control. Thank you for your help.

Sample Letter 2 (urgent request):

Dear Sir:

This is the third reminder we have sent you regarding your past due account. As a professional, we know this is an avoidable dilemma. The key is to make this matter a priority by giving it your full attention.

Our position on this issue has not changed. We insist that your account be brought up to date as soon as possible. Do not waste any more valuable time; your lack of answer is destroying any possibility of future business with us. We hope to hear from you within the next week with confirmation that the problem has been settled to our mutual satisfaction.

OPTIONAL WRITING PRACTICE

Practice A. Write a letter of acknowledgment for a check you just received. Specify that the amount of the check was incorrect and give the correct amount.

Practice B. Write a collection letter for a customer who hasn't sent in his last three payments on his real estate loan. Give him a maximum of 15 days to bring his account up to date, before legal action is taken.

Practice C. Answer the letter from Sample 2 above specifying why payment has not been made and when it can be expected.

Practice D. Answer the letter from Sample 1 on the previous page.

Letter of Remittance (or Transmittal)

This type of letter is used when you send a check or any other important document by mail. It is a way of letting the recipient know exactly what he or she is supposed to receive.

Follow these guidelines when preparing a letter of remittance:

- Ö Identify what it is that you are sending.
- Ö Specify the amount of the check, if any.
- Ö Identify the purpose for the remittance: payment on an invoice, for a specific account, etc.

Sample Letter

Dear Sir:

    Due to the nature of our business, we require final approval of all media placements before publication. Should you receive any sales inquiries during the term of our contract, please refer them to Mrs. Glendy Settinlove, Sales Manager.

    In the meantime, we are sending check AB234 for the amount of $984.24 to cover the initial fees we agreed upon. We are also enclosing a copy of the contract to review and sign . We look forward to a long and rewarding relationship with your organization.

Practice A: Write a letter acknowledging the receipt of the items mentioned in the sample letter above.

Practice B. Write a remittance letter to be sent with three sound systems which are being shipped immediately.

Claim Letter

This is a letter which companies hate to receive, because it means that the customer isn't happy with the merchandise or services received.

When you write a letter of claim, try to follow these rules:

Ö Explain clearly and tactfully what is wrong.
Ö Include all the necessary information (dates, account or product numbers, etc.)
Ö Indicate the inconvenience you have suffered.
Ö Explain what you want the company to do, but be reasonable.
Ö Do not accuse. Always assume that the mistake was NOT intentional.

Sample Letter

Dear Mrs. Bettis:

We received the bill for your services regarding the recent contract negotiations which have just concluded. Upon checking the bill, however, we found that the total almost doubles the original amount agreed upon. Perhaps we have simply had a misunderstanding over fees and expenses, or perhaps our records have somehow been confused with those of another organization. Please review the bill for any possible adjustments and advise us of your position as soon as possible.

Thank you for your professional courtesy in this matter. Anything you can do to reduce the total is greatly appreciated.

Adjustment Letter

An adjustment letter is the response to a claim letter. In some ways, therefore, it is similar to a letter of acknowledgment.

A letter of adjustment should be sent as soon as the complaint is received. In it, you must show the customer that you understand the situation and explain what you are going to do to solve the problem. It is essential that you avoid negative words or expressions.

Sample Letter

Dear Mr. Jacobs:

> After extensive review of your complaint, we have no alternative but to admit that our shipping department mishandled your order. The entire staff has been so professional in the past that this unfortunate incident came as a total surprise to all of us.
>
> We understand that your organization has the right to file a formal complaint with the Small Business Administration. However, we hope that this matter can be properly settled among ourselves without the need for outside intervention.
>
> Thank you for all you have done to strenghthen our business relationship. If you need further assistance, please do not hesitate to contact us.

Practice 1. Write the Letter of Claim which is answered in the sample letter above. Essentially, you are complaining about an order which did not arrive when it was supposed to. Specify dates, merchandise, amounts, etc.

The Interoffice Memorandum

Memos are sent to people who work in your own company, either in the same building or out of it. Most companies have their own printed forms to be used when sending a memo.

Regardless of the form used, most memos have three parts:

- The heading
- The subject
- The message

Note: the plural of memorandum is memoranda, but **memorandums** is widely used.

Sample Memo Headings

INTEROFFICE MEMORANDUM		
TO:	*(addressee)*	**DATE:**
FROM:	*(sender)*	
SUBJECT:	*(reason for the memo)*	

MEMORANDUM		
To:	*(Addressee)*	**Date:**
From:	*(Sender)*	
Re:	*(Regarding)*	

The message usually has three parts.

- Reasons for the memo
- Detailed information
- Suggestions or requests for future action

Business English and Conversation - Armando Aceituno M.

Interoffice memoranda are not usually signed, but this is left to the writer's preference.

One important aspect to remember is that memos should be short and to the point. They are documents which are used to handle the communication within an organization, but should be used with a lot of care.

Sample Memo

TO: Francis Dawson, Sales Manager
DATE: 07-15-2001
FROM: Jennie Piccolo, General Manager
SUBJECT: Absenteeism

At the last general meeting, it was mentioned that absenteeism in all departments has risen this year to an all time high. This problem, however, seems to be hitting especially the Sales Department, and that is a situation which could lead to further short and long term difficulties.

Please take all the necessary steps to ensure that absenteeism in your department is reduced to a minimum. We do not want to reach the point at which stronger actions are necessary

Practice. Write a memorandum to your staff congratulating them on a job well done during the holiday season. Mention a bonus to be awarded to each staff member according to seniority.

Letter of Reference

A letter of reference is given to someone who is known personally to the one preparing it. In some countries, however, most large companies do not give them anymore. They provide only certain information about a former employee, and they do this usually by telephone rather than by mail.

When you write a letter of reference try to adhere to the following guidelines:

1. Don't write it for just anyone
2. Be careful what you say about that person
3. Do not provide confidential information unless it is required by the situation. (legal requirement, government dealings, applying for credit, etc.)

Sample Letter

TO WHOM IT MAY CONCERN

This is to certify that I have known Mrs. Wendy Walters since 1999, when she worked for my organization as an account executive.

During the time Mrs. Walters worked for this organization, she proved to be a valuable asset. Her work was always of high quality and her human relations were also above reproach.

I recommend Mrs. Walters without reservation.

Practice. Write a letter of reference for an ex-employee of your company. Be careful with the information you provide.

Telegram

In some areas of the world, this means of communication is not used anymore, since we now have fax and e-mail. However, if you do need to send a telegram, it should be very brief; the message must be stated in as few words as possible.

Sample Telegram

> FOUND MISSING DOCUMENTS. SENDING AIR MAIL NEXT WEEK.

Notice that we eliminate most nonessential words. The normal message might read as follows:

> We found the documents which were missing. We are sending them by air mail next week.

Practice A. Write a telegram announcing a meeting. Give date and time.

Practice B. Write a telegram asking for confirmation of a conference.

Practice C. Write a telegram telling the addressee that the money has been deposited in the bank. Give the account number in which the money was deposited.

Résumé

Your confidential résumé is an important document, since it tells the world about who you are. The format you choose may vary, and even the information you include will vary from time to time and from country to country. But there are certain standard information most people include:

Personal information:
    Name
    Address
    Birthdate
    Birthplace
    Phone No.
    Identification number, Passport, etc.)
    Social Security Number *

Education:
    Elementary (Grade) school
    High School (or other studies)
    College or University degree
    Other training courses or seminars

Employment history:
    Last job held
    Name of the company
    Last position held
    Salary *
    Responsibilities

Special skills:
    Typing speed
    Fluency in other languages
    Computer ability

Hobbies
Other information
Personal References *

* Optional

Appendix A | Useful Business Phrases

1. Will you please send me information on...
2. I would appreciate your sending me information...
3. Please send me the following information...
4. Thank you for your prompt reply.
5. I will appreciate your response.
6. Please send the information to...
7. Please send your reply to...
8. Would you please send me a copy of your magazine.
9. We need the following supplies:
10. A self-addressed envelope is enclosed for your convenience.
11. Please return the receipt with your signature.
12. Please return the reply card.
13. A copy of the advertisement is enclosed.
14. Please sign the original and return it to...
15. The enclosed questionnaire should be completed and returned.
16. As soon as possible.
17. At your earliest convenience.
18. Thank you for your letter of September 1.
19. Thank you for your check for $74.25.
20. We appreciate your interest in our products.
21. We received your letter dated August 1.
22. Take advantage of our special promotion.
23. Our company does not deal with those products.
24. Prices have been drastically lowered.
25. We are offering a 20% discount on all purchases.
26. Thank you for your recent request.
27. Thank you for your order of May 3.
28. Thank you for your order for a Supertrack Lawn Mower.
29. We are pleased to have your order.
30. We are sending you a free sample of...
31. We are glad to have your business.
32. Your order is being processed.
33. Your order will be shipped on April 20.
34. We were delighted to receive your order (or request)
35. We hope to be of service to you.

36. You are welcome to visit our showroom at (address)
37. Thank you for writing about the...
38. We are sending you a brochure with complete details.
39. A free booklet is enclosed.
40. Your request has been referred to our Houston Office.
41. The processing of your order dated January 2, has been delayed.
42. Most of your questions are answered in the enclosed booklet.
43. May we urge you to make your reservations early.
44. Thank you for your prompt attention to our request.
45. Our manager, Mr. Roberts, will get in touch with you.
46. Our order dated July 29, arrived today.
47. We hope to hear from you immediately regarding this situation.
48. We received ... instead of the ... specified in our order.
49. We shall appreciate your promptness in correcting this error.
50. Thank you for giving this matter your full attention.
51. The merchandise arrived incomplete.
52. The numbers on the items do not match those of the invoice.
53. We will take whatever steps are necessary to correct this problem.
54. A refund in the amount of $43.98 is being sent to you.
55. Your check number 3442 in the amount of $345.44 has been rejected due to insufficient funds.
56. Your account has been credited for the full amount.
57. The merchandise will be replaced at no cost to you.
58. We are pleased to replace the defective merchandise.
59. Due to unforeseen circumstances...
60. Circumstances beyond our control...
61. We are unable to fill your order...
62. Thank you for calling our attention to...
63. Thank you for your suggestions concerning...
64. Your account is overdue...
65. The payment due on July 13, has not been received.
66. If your payment has been made, please disregard this notice.
67. Unless your account is paid by (date), it will be turned over to a collection agency.
68. We appreciate your cooperation in this matter.
69. Thank you for your check in the amount of $332.87.
70. Your check for $787.76 has been received.
71. Will you please send us the balance due before March 13.
72. Unfortunately, your order cannot be filled, since...
73. The items you requested are out of stock.
74. If you need more information, please call us at (number)
75. ... do not hesitate to call us.

Appendix B | Regular Verbs

We cannot include all the regular and irregular verbs due to space limitations. Consult your dictionary to verify whether a verb is regular or irregular.

absorb	assist	chew	darken
abuse	assure	clean	dawn
accede	attain	climb	deceive
accept	attempt	close	decide
accommodate	attend	collect	declare
accompany	auction	comb	decompose
accomplish	augment	command	decrease
accustom	avoid	commence	deduce
ache	await	comment	deepen
acknowledge	bake	compare	defeat
add	bathe	compel	defend
adjourn	beautify	compensate	defer
admire	behave	complain	defray
admit	believe	compliment	delay
adore	belong	conceal	deliberate
adorn	better	confide	deliver
advance	bless	confuse	demonstrate
advertise	blossom	correspond	deny
advise	blot	consecrate	depose
affect	blush	consent	deposit
afford	boast	consume	depreciate
affront	boil	content	deprive
aid	bore	cook	derive
allude	bother	cough	derogate
alternate	breathe	count	descend
amuse	brush	cover	desert
announce	burn	covet	deserve
annoy	bury	cross	desire
answer	button	crush	desist
appeal	call	cry	despair
appear	care	cure	despise
appreciate	carry	curl	destroy
arrange	cease	curse	detain
arrest	challenge	dampen	deteriorate
arrive	change	dance	detest
ask	cheer	dare	dethrone

179

develop	exhibit	import	like
die	exist	improve	limp
differ	expectorate	include	line
diminish	expel	increase	listen
dine	fail	incur	live
direct	faint	infer	load
dirty	fancy	infest	lodge
disappear	fear	inform	look
disconcert	fill	inhabit	loose
discount	finish	initiate	love
discourse	fire	innovate	maintain
disguise	fish	inquire	manage
disinherit	fix	insert	manifest
dismiss	flatter	insist	match
disobey	flood	inspire	mate
dispose	fold	instruct	mediate
distinguish	follow	intercede	meditate
distract	foment	interpret	melt
distribute	free	interrogate	mend
distrust	fret	interrupt	milk
divide	fry	introduce	miss
doubt	furnish	inundate	mix
dream	gain	invent	mock
dress	gamble	invert	moisten
drizzle	gape	iron	molest
drop	gather	itch	mortgage
drown	gaze	jest	mount
dry	gild	join	mourn
dye	glitter	joke	move
effect	glue	judge	multiply
elect	govern	jump	nail
embalm	grant	kick	name
embrace	grasp	kill	navigate
emit	greet	kiss	need
emphasize	groan	knock	neglect
employ	hail	knot	nod
empty	hand	lack	nourish
endure	hang	lament	obey
enjoy	happen	land	observe
enter	hate	languish	obstruct
entreat	heal	last	obtain
envy	heat	laugh	occasion
erase	help	lean	occupy
escape	hire	learn	occur
estimate	humor	lick	offend
excuse	hunt	lie	offer
exercise	imitate	light	omit

open	procure	rest	sneeze
oppose	produce	retire	snore
oppress	profess	return	snow
order	proffer	revolve	soak
overturn	prohibit	reward	sob
owe	project	ripen	soil
pain	promise	roast	solder
paint	propose	rock	solve
pardon	protest	roll	sound
participate	prove	rot	sow
pass	provide	row	spatter
pave	publish	rule	speculate
pawn	pull	salt	spell
pay	punish	save	spill
peep	push	scatter	spin
perform	rage	scold	split
perish	rain	scratch	spoil
permit	raise	scream	sprinkle
persecute	ransack	scrub	squeeze
perspire	rave	seal	stain
pervert	reach	season	step
pet	reap	separate	stoop
pierce	recite	serve	stop
pinch	recommend	settle	straighten
place	refer	shake	stretch
plant	reflect	shame	struggle
play	refresh	sharpen	study
plead	reign	shave	stumble
please	rejoice	shelter	stutter
plot	relapse	ship	subdue
plough	relate	shiver	submerge
populate	relieve	shock	subtract
possess	remain	show	suffer
post	remember	sigh	suggest
postpone	remind	sign	supply
pound	remove	silence	support
praise	renovate	sin	suppose
pray	rent	singe	surprise
preach	repeat	sip	suspect
predict	repel	skate	suspend
prefer	repent	sketch	swallow
prepare	request	slip	swindle
present	resemble	smell	talk
press	resent	smile	tame
pretend	resist	smoke	taste
print	resolve	smooth	tempt
proceed	respect	smother	thank

181

threaten
thunder
tickle
tie
tighten
tire
toast
touch
trace
trade
transfer
translate
transpire
transpose
travel
traverse
treat
tremble
trip
trust
try
tune
twist
undertake
unite
use
value
vanquish
varnish
vary
vegetate
venerate
ventilate
verify
vex
violate
whisper
visit
wait
walk
waltz
wander
want
warn
wash
waste
watch

weep
weigh
wet
whistle
whitewash
will
wish
wonder
work

worry
wound
wrap
wreck
wrinkle
yawn
yield
zip
zoom

Appendix C — Irregular Verbs

BASE FORM	PAST FORM	PAST PARTICIPLE (with HAVE or HAS)
abide	abode	abode
arise	arose	arisen
awake	awoke	awaked
be	was/were	been
bear	bore	born
beat	beat	beat
become	became	become
begin	began	begun
bend	bent	bent
bet	bet	bet
bid (offer)	bid	bid
bid (order)	bade	bidden
bind	bound	bound
bite	bit	bitten
bleed	bled	bled
blow	blew	blown
break	broke	broken
breed	bred	bred
bring	brought	brought
build	built	built
burn	burned	burnt
burst	burst	burst
buy	bought	bought
cast	cast	cast
catch	caught	caught
choose	chose	chosen
cling	clung	clung

clothe	clothed/clad	clothed/clad		**lend**	lent	lent
come	came	come		**let**	let	let
cost	cost	cost		**lie**	lay	lain
creep	crept	crept		**light**	lit	lit
cut	cut	cut		**lose**	lost	lost
deal	dealt	dealt		**make**	made	made
dig	dug	dug		**mean**	meant	meant
dive	dove	dived		**meet**	met	met
do	did	done		**mistake**	mistook	mistaken
draw	drew	drawn		**pay**	paid	paid
dream	dreamed	dreamed/dreamt		**plead**	pled	pled
drink	drank	drunk		**prove**	proved	proven
drive	drove	driven		**put**	put	put
dwell	dwelt	dwelt		**quit**	quit	quit
eat	ate	eaten		**read**	read	read
fall	fell	fallen		**ride**	rode	ridden
feed	fed	fed		**ring**	rang	rung
feel	felt	felt		**rise**	rose	risen
fight	fought	fought		**run**	ran	run
find	found	found		**say**	said	said
flee	fled	fled		**see**	saw	seen
fling	flung	flung		**seek**	sought	sought
fly	flew	flown		**sell**	sold	sold
forbid	forbade	forbidden		**send**	sent	sent
forget	forgot	forgotten		**set**	set	set
forgive	forgave	forgiven		**shake**	shook	shaken
forsake	forsook	forsaken		**shave**	shaved	shaved/shaven
freeze	froze	frozen		**shed**	shed	shed
get	got	gotten		**shine**	shone/shined	shone/shined
give	gave	given		**shoot**	shot	shot
go	went	gone		**show**	showed	shown
grind	ground	ground		**shred**	shred	shred
grow	grew	grown		**shrink**	shrank	shrunk
hang	hung	hung		**shut**	shut	shut
have	had	had		**sing**	sang	sung
hear	heard	heard		**sink**	sank	sunk
hide	hid	hidden		**sit**	sat	sat
hit	hit	hit		**slay**	slew	slain
hold	held	held		**sleep**	slept	slept
hurt	hurt	hurt		**slide**	slid	slid/slidden
keep	kept	kept		**slit**	slit	slit
kneel	knelt	knelt		**smite**	smote	smitten
knit	knit	knit		**sow**	sowed	sown
know	knew	known		**speak**	spoke	spoken
lay	laid	laid		**speed**	sped	sped
lead	led	led		**spend**	spent	spent
leave	left	left		**spin**	spun	spun

spit	spit	spit
split	split	split
spread	spread	spread
spring	sprang	sprung
stand	stood	stood
steal	stole	stolen
stick	stuck	stuck
sting	stung	stung
stink	stunk	stunk
strike	struck	struck
swear	swore	sworn
sweat	sweat	sweat
sweep	swept	swept
swell	swelled	swollen
swim	swam	swum
swing	swung	swung
take	took	taken
teach	taught	taught
tear	tore	torn
tell	told	told
think	thought	thought
throw	threw	thrown
thrust	thrust	thrust
understand	understood	understood
wake	woke	waked/woken
wear	wore	worn
weave	wove	woven
weep	wept	wept
win	won	won
wind	wound	wound
withdraw	withdrew	withdrawn
withstand	withstood	withstood
wring	wrung	wrung
write	wrote	written

Printed in the United States
2884

9 781581 127126